Beth
Doctor Gibbons

With love
from
Melanie Gibbons

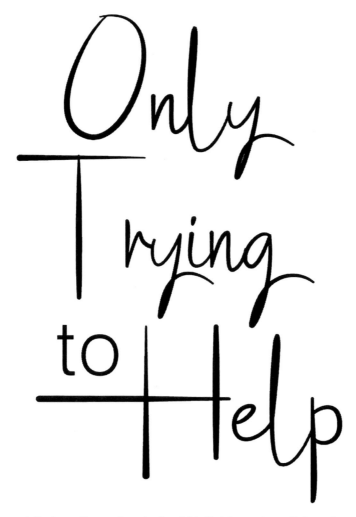

Higher Standards for Well-Meaning Friends,
Colleagues, Parents, and Partners

By Dr. Kate Watson

Published by Dr. Kathleen Watson, The Advocacy Academy, LLC

Philadelphia, PA | United States of America

Copyright © 2020 by Dr. Kathleen Watson

ISBN print 978-1-09836-674-2 | ISBN eBook 978-1-09836-675-9

1st Edition

All rights reserved. No part of this publication may be reproduced, distributed, or transmitted in any form or by any means, including photocopying, recording, or other electronic or mechanical methods, without the prior written permission of the publisher, except in the case of brief quotations embodied in critical reviews and certain other non-commercial uses permitted by copyright law.

For permission requests, contact Kate@OnlyTryingToHelp.com.

For speaker inquiries, contact Kate@AdvocacyAcademy.org.

Book Cover Design Draft: Nicole Greenberg

Book Cover Design Final: Book Baby, LLC.

Illustrations: Laura Stewart

Ordering Available at:

www.OnlyTryingToHelp.com

www.AdvocacyAcademy.org

www.Amazon.com

Dedication

Dedicated to Jeremy, who always means well (except, of course, for when he doesn't).

Disclaimer

This book is not intended to give health or mental health advice. If you or someone you know is experiencing a physical or mental health crisis, please call 911. Names, personal information, and other details have been altered to protect the privacy of individuals.

Acknowledgements

Thank you to those who loyally follow and support the podcast week-by-week: Dave Jacowitz, Leah Temple, Alex Temple, Alyson Kelly, and Mats Hogmark.

Thank you to Laura Stewart and Nicole Greenberg for assisting me with artwork and design.

Thank you to my She Means Business group members: Mallori DeSalle, Katie Hartlieb, and Jennifer Ollis Blomqvist. Each of you supported my progress over the past year.

Thank you my closest friends, Julie Gehring, Claire Lane, and Debra Temple. The three of you are kind enough that you don't hold me to the standards I've outlined in this book. With each of you, I can make a million mistakes.

Also, I owe infinite thanks to Leslie Ballway, who is my friend, the co-host of our internationally known podcast, and my sister for life.

In my mind, *Only Trying to Help* was always going to be a book. I started the podcast only as a test lab for potential book material. I invited Leslie to join me on this adventure because I trusted her intellect and humor. I never could have imagined that the podcast would run for multiple seasons and reach listeners in thirty countries around the world. Her insight and authenticity are the music to my lyrics. I bring the information, and she brings the unscripted humanity.

Finally, I'd like to thank Eileen Scully Ballway for raising Leslie to be the wisecracking, independent, and empathic soul that she is. Eileen passed away while I was writing this book, but Leslie's contributions cement Eileen's legacy.

Contents

Acknowledgements i

Introduction 1

Chapter 1: Well-Meaning Encouragement 17

Chapter 2: Well-Meaning Compliments 38

Chapter 3: Well-Meaning Apologies..50

Chapter 4: Well-Meaning Advice 58

Chapter 5: Well-Meaning Tough Love..70

Chapter 6: Well-Meaning Humor 86

Chapter 7: Well-Meaning Gift Giving...96

Chapter 8: Well-Meaning Lies 104

Conclusion 110

Afterword: Publishing in the COVID Era 112

Resources.. 114

Appendix A: Tips for Effective Self-Disclosure............................ 116

Appendix B: Examples of Boundaries 118

Appendix C: Emotional Vocabulary.. 122

Appendix D: Microaggressions 131

About the Author 134

Introduction

> *No one is useless in this world who
> lightens the burdens of another.*
> — *Charles Dickens*

For at least a portion of my childhood, my father tended bar for a hotel restaurant in Philadelphia. Given that his tenure lasted through the mid- to late 1980s, it should be no surprise that he had a thick mustache and poured his fair share of neon-colored cocktails. This was over thirty years ago, so I have long forgotten most details about the restaurant décor, the music on the stereo, and the fashions of the clientele, but I have vivid memories of watching him behind the bar, leaning against the polished oak, while I ate my weight in maraschino cherries and dangled my five-year-old legs from the barstool. I embodied Norm from *Cheers* before kindergarten, so no wonder I was such a fat kid while growing up.

Thirty or forty years prior to that, probably around the time my dad was born, my great-grandfather was a barber for the locals in his Philadelphia neighborhood. I obviously never had the chance to witness him cut hair, but to this day, sitting on my dad's basement office desk is a framed photo of my great-grandfather cutting his daughter's (my grandmother Dolores's) hair in his barbershop in the 1950s. I know the image so well. He is only half smiling, like he knows the camera is watching and he is thinking the "photo op" is ridiculous and embarrassing. If that photo had sound effects, you'd hear a person saying, "Come on, give a smile for the camera," and my great-grandfather would say, "Ah, geez, would youse get out here with that." Still, he smiled.

These men—my dad and his grandfather—were there to serve others, whether with cocktails, hot towels, or the inevitable relationship advice. They were helpers. Sometimes I like to imagine that, over the years, my great-grandfather hosted hundreds, maybe thousands, of customers who came for a shave and a hot towel and to talk about their troubles, just as my dad hosted many travelers and strangers in the hotel bar of the Marriott Courtyard on City Line Avenue decades later. Both barbers and bartenders feel like American archetypes of brotherly love, not just in Philadelphia, where my family's story is rooted, but in all corners of our country. The bartender who says, "Tell me your troubles" is, frankly, my earliest memory of friendship and kindness between adults.

So clearly, I'm not the first therapist in my family. I'm just, after thirty years of education and $100,000 in student loans, the first well-trained therapist in the family (sorry, Dad). But if you think about it, informal counselors lurk around every corner, and most of them didn't get a degree or a fancy credential. It isn't just the bartenders and barbers who hear about the troubles of the world but also teachers, coaches, neighbors, and colleagues we find at the watercooler. This book is for them: the everyday therapists and advisors among us. This is a book for people who like to help others but are tired of screwing it all up. They're tired of feeling useless. They're tired of throwing their arms in the air in exhaustion and claiming, "I'm only trying to help!"

Sure, the mom who completes her son's book report is only trying to help. The coach who screams, "You can do better than that!" at an athlete who lost the game is only trying to help. The friend who says, "That guy is no good for you. You need to leave his ass!" is also only trying to help. The sister who casually says, "You should try Weight Watchers. It worked for my friend" is only trying to help. This book is for the people who want to confidently support a friend who has been diagnosed with cancer. This book is for the people who want to help loved ones grieve the loss of jobs, pets, marriages, and parents. This book merges what I learned over many years of advanced education with what I probably picked up from the bartenders and barbers in my bloodline to help you help others more effectively. I like to think of these highly researched skills as a form of scientific kindness.

Together, we will walk through eight chapters of well-meaning attempts at help:

- Chapter 1: Well-Meaning Encouragement
- Chapter 2: Well-Meaning Compliments
- Chapter 3: Well-Meaning Apologies
- Chapter 4: Well-Meaning Advice
- Chapter 5: Well-Meaning Tough Love
- Chapter 6: Well-Meaning Humor
- Chapter 7: Well-Meaning Gift Giving
- Chapter 8: Well-Meaning Lies

Within each chapter, you will find stories of success and failure, academic research, and tips for improving your relationships through communication, patience, and empathy. But before we dive into these categories together, I would like to introduce some themes so you can track them throughout the book. Call them the new standards of helpfulness, if you will.

Standard #1: Listen More Than You Speak

Take five minutes to peruse some online dating profiles and you will quickly notice that every prospect describes himself or herself as down to earth, funny, nonjudgmental, and a great listener. Horseshit. There are some qualities we like to *think* we possess, but let's be honest: We are not all funny. We are not all down to earth. I've never met a person free of judgment. Even though my social circle includes hundreds of therapists and social workers, I know maybe three or four people who are truly good listeners.

My point is that listening is a skill to be practiced with diligence. It is selfless and extraordinary when someone takes the time to listen and understand because it requires you to suspend your own need to feel clever, constructive, and consequential. It's also a really nice thing to do, dammit!

Here is the problem. Too often we try to connect with other people by talking about ourselves more than we listen, and I can identify at least four major problems with that.

1. It robs the attention from the person you are trying to help.
2. It dismisses the point of the person you are trying to help.
3. The person you are trying to help feels obligated to take care of you rather than receive your support and love.
4. You, the helper, stop listening.

A few months ago, I had a conversation with my friend Rob about my goals for health and wellness. He and I are both goal-oriented people, and we hold each other accountable in a way that doesn't feel invasive or annoying (which is a high compliment from me since I'm an introvert and I find a lot of people invasive and annoying).

I said to Rob, "I might try intermittent fasting. It could be great for my weight loss goals. I probably need to ease into it though. I can't just wake up tomorrow and implement this immediately, but I'm excited to try it."

He looked excited too, and I thought he would say something like "Wow, that's so great. Keep me posted. I'd love to hear how you feel when you get started." Instead, like he hadn't even heard me, he said, "I was thinking about cutting sugar out of my diet. I really think I need to look at that. I'm going to meet with a nutritionist and see what that's all about. I've gotta lose these last ten pounds!"

My gut instinct, as a counselor, good listener, good friend, and overall decent human being, was to show some interest in what he said. Theoretically, if I had followed that instinct, I would have said, "Sugar, huh? Good for you! That sounds really difficult." But I didn't want to say that. I hadn't finished my conversation about intermittent fasting. Eff sugar. I wasn't sure if he had even heard me. So I said, "Well, I think the intermittent fasting will give me the sense of control that I like to feel. I thrive on that."

I had hoped he might take the hint that I was trying to focus the conversation back on me. I mean, after all, I had initiated the conversation. Don't I get at least five minutes of his attention?

To my disappointment, he said, "I don't need a sense of control. I just need to see results, and that will keep me motivated. The nutritionist will help me with that. I'm probably going to meet with him on Friday. Oh, shit, I have that other meeting on Friday! I will have to reschedule."

We went several repetitive rounds like this—with me trying to talk about myself and him trying to do the same. I won't bore you with the details, but I was fuming. I imagined that we were performers on a stage, but there was only one spotlight, and we were fighting over the audience's attention. Every time I stepped into the spotlight, it felt like he pushed me out to make room for himself.

I eventually just bluntly asked him, "Did you even hear what I said about intermittent fasting? Are you following me at all?"

He looked at me like I was being childish. He said, "Yeah, of course. I just wanted to share my ideas too. I thought we were having a conversation."

In one of those laugh-to-keep-from-crying moments, I burst out in a cantankerous chuckle. After composing myself a little, I said, "All I'm asking for is some acknowledgment you heard me before you just start talking about yourself. And yes, I acknowledge a conversation is about two people sharing ideas together. But a conversation is also composed of both listeners and speakers. When I speak, you're the listener, and when you speak, I'm the listener."

He looked hurt. Had I said too much? Maybe we didn't have the kind of relationship where I could be so honest. Then I slowed down for a second and added, "Look, you are very good at the speaking part, and I am very good at the listening part. But let's not get stuck in those roles permanently because it's not fair to me. I need a friend."

I think he understood for the moment, but those habits are hard to break in a long-term, meaningful way (unless you practice with sincerity).

In fact, I once spoke about this topic to a large audience and, during the Q and A portion, a person asked me, "But if I'm not talking about myself, how am I being helpful?" Now, hoping to uphold some sense of professionalism, I knew I could not tell her how arrogant it is to believe that your only hope for helping people is to talk about your damn self. *Who the hell do you think you are?*

To make yourself the center of every interaction is conversational narcissism. So please listen with a kind and curious heart and try to calm your urges to talk so much. There isn't anyone you couldn't learn to love once you've heard their story, but you have to listen. I'll tell you, one of my favorite quotes comes from Garth Stein, who wrote *The Art of Racing in the Rain*. He wrote, "Here's why I will be a good person. Because I listen. I cannot speak, so I listen very well. I never interrupt, I never deflect the course of the conversation with a comment of my own. People, if you pay attention to them, change the direction of one another's conversations constantly. It's like having a passenger in your car who suddenly grabs the steering wheel and turns you down a side street."

Folks, I know you think it's helpful to talk a lot, but please keep in mind a key thing: There is a big difference between feeling helpful and being helpful. Self-disclosure often feels helpful, but shutting the eff up is helpful.

Let's do a little test:

1. On a scale of 1 to 10, how important is it to you to *feel* helpful to others? (10 = it's the most important thing in the world to you, 1 = it's the least important thing in the world to you)

1	2	3	4	5	6	7	8	9	10

2. On a scale of 1 to 10, how important is it to you to *be* helpful to others? (10 = it's the most important thing in the world to you, 1 = it's the least important thing in the world to you)

1	2	3	4	5	6	7	8	9	10

If your answer to number 1 is a higher number than your answer to number 2, you should just put this book away. You're not ready for it. Go have a margarita and watch Netflix instead.

It's not that self-disclosure is completely off the table. But there is a way to do it that is more effective than just blurting out shit that pertains only to you. See Appendix A for some tips about how to self-disclose without harming the conversation.

And for now, remember what jazz musician Dizzy Gillespie famously said, "It's taken me my whole life to learn what not to play." Choose your words carefully, friends. Learn what *not* to play.

Standard #2: Assert and Respect Boundaries

For most of my youth and young adult years, I dieted—sometimes in unhealthy and extreme ways. I would lose twenty to forty pounds and then gain it back. Repeat. Repeat again. A person doesn't yo-yo diet that much without learning a thing or two about themselves.

I realized I had a lot of unproductive patterns that I needed to break. I would, for example, set goals for healthy eating and then violate my own intentions in social settings, citing concern for others. It would sound like this in my head: "I told myself I would just drink water with my meal tonight, but people get weird about alcohol. They're going to feel strange ordering cocktails, if I'm not joining them." Then I would drink alcohol to make everyone else comfortable.

If I had intended to order a salad from the menu, I would suddenly think, "Everyone else ordered burgers. They will feel bad about themselves if I order a salad. I should at least get some french fries so they don't feel judged by me." Sometimes, when the meal would end, people would say things like "Oh, come on, share the dessert with me. Don't make me eat it all by myself." And I'd eat it to make them feel better.

I would work so hard to lose weight, just to gain it all back because I didn't want to make other people uncomfortable. That is an example of embarrassingly poor boundaries. Boundaries are the separation between what belongs to me and what belongs to you. In this case, my food decisions belonged to me, and other people are responsible for their own food decisions. It wasn't up to me to help other people feel comfortable with their drinking or red meat or dessert. I was crossing boundaries, and meanwhile, I was congratulating myself for being helpful and considerate. I had to learn that I am not responsible for the guilt or shame that belongs to other people, putting down, once and for all, the weight that was never really mine to carry in the first place.

There are endless examples of well-meaning helpers exhausting themselves because they lack the boundaries to know where and when the help must end. Having a big heart will often leave you feeling like you did either too much or not enough. For that reason, boundaries are a major theme of this book. Standard #2 is that we all need to assert our own boundaries, and we need to respect the boundaries of others. My feelings belong to me, and your feelings belong to you. My time belongs to me, and your time belongs to you. My property belongs to me, and your property belongs to you. My rights belong to me, and your rights belong to you. The key message is "Separate what you have power over and what you do not have power over because some of us are trying to fix things we have no control over at all. Stop it."

When I work with clients who are struggling with boundaries, I help them complete a table that mirrors the one you see below. Here, I've shared an example of how one client described the boundaries she needed to set with her romantic partner.

	Within My Boundaries	Outside of My Boundaries
Time	I decide how I will spend my time.	My partner's stress and projects will not dictate my schedule. His deadlines belong to him, not me.
Rights	I have the right to peace. I have the right to happiness. I have the right to safety.	I do not need to compromise my peace, happiness, or safety to accommodate my partner.
Responsibilities	My responsibilities include paying my bills, taking care of my health, meeting my deadlines, and completing my goals.	My partner's responsibilities include parenting his child from a previous marriage, managing his money, and completing his goals and deadlines. These things are not my responsibility.
Property	My things belong to me. I own them. I need to take care of them. That's my job.	I am not responsible for my partner's property.
Beliefs	My spiritual and intellectual beliefs are my own. I do not need to defend them.	I cannot control my partner's beliefs. He can vote for whomever he chooses, and he can believe whatever he wants to believe. It's not up to me.

Physical Space	My body belongs to me.	My partner cannot demand or expect sex from me when I'm not interested in it. I am not responsible for his urges.
Emotions	I manage my own emotions. No one can do that on my behalf.	My partner has to manage his own emotions. I cannot do that on his behalf.
Energy	I am in control of my energy. I am responsible for the energy I bring into a room.	My partner may not be energized by the same things that energize me. I am not responsible for managing his energy.

Let's be clear: You can't change people. That, my friend, is outside of your boundaries. But you can *help* people by changing your approach with them. The point is to stay focused on your own behavior and watch people heal as a result. If you manage your tone of voice and your body language and you choose your words carefully, the people in your life will benefit from feeling understood and loved. I'm going to teach you how to do that. But as you know, changing yourself is hard. If it were so easy to manage my own behavior, I would have gone to the gym today, and I would have eaten a healthier lunch. Remember how difficult it is to change yourself when you're exhausted trying to change others.

This book is not about getting your friends to lose weight or to leave their husbands or to start that business or to quit drinking. This book is about changing your responses and reactions to the people you want to help. Let me repeat that—I know you want to help other people have glorious lives, but this book is about changing yourself so you stand a chance of being helpful to them. You want to help your parents get healthy? Don't change them. Change your approach. You want to help your son become more social? Don't change him. Change your approach. You want to help your best friend escape a horrible marriage? Don't change her. Change your approach. You want to help your spouse go back to school? Don't change your spouse. Change your approach. That is how you help people within your own boundaries.

Throughout this book, you will read that we ought to consider the feelings and experiences of other people. Please don't confuse that with trying to fix or change people. Considering how a person might feel is kind, but trying to fix how the person feels is not going to work. You can't control another person's feelings, experiences, or even behaviors, but you can consider them and respect them. Caring about a person's feelings is not the same as feeling responsible for them.

We learn about feelings in kindergarten, and then we barely hear about them again for the rest of our lives. So in case you need a little kindergarten refresher, I included a list of emotional vocabulary words in Appendix C of this book.

Standard #3: Forgive Yourself for Not Reading Minds

I read a fascinating book by Nicholas Epley called *Mindwise: How We Understand What Others Think, Believe, Feel, and Want*. The book's message was clear: We don't know shit about other people. But even though Epley has mountains of research to show us we are inaccurate when we try to guess how people think and feel, he insists that we try anyway. He claims we *are* mind readers—just not very good ones.

When we, for example, send flowers to a grieving friend, we make a guess about what they would want to read on the card. That's an attempt at mind reading, and we could certainly get it wrong. When we see a coworker eating lunch alone, we might guess that he or she would like some company. That's an attempt at mind reading, and it could be immensely inaccurate.

So even though we are going to review many tools for compassionate communication, at the end of the day, I don't really know what will work for you in your life and in your relationships. I don't know what your loved ones need and want from you. I can't read minds. Neither can you. And no one is expecting you to read minds accurately. A key message of this book is that you might make some attempts to read minds, you might get it wrong, and if you're really worried about it, just ask people what they need. Let me repeat that—just ask people what they need.

I recently read an article in *The Atlantic* (Eichler, 2010) that helped me understand the important difference between asking and guessing in relationships. Apparently, some people were raised in a home where it was appropriate to ask for just about anything, but they had to be prepared for the response to be a firm no. *May I have pizza for breakfast? No. May I take the bus into the city by myself? No. May I skip school tomorrow? No.*

For askers, the best way to navigate the world is to ask for the things you need and the answers you don't yet have. Simple. Just ask.

I didn't grow up in a house like this. I grew up in a home full of signals and subtleties where we were expected to only ask for things if the answer was reasonably likely to be yes. *I'm not even going to ask Mom and Dad if I can I have some money because I'm pretty sure the answer is no. I'm not even going to ask Mom and Dad if I can stay out beyond curfew because I'm pretty sure the answer is no.* We were supposed to use our instincts and experience to guess the answers to our questions. By doing so, we avoided any risk of bothering a person with a silly question. Epley would say that we were expected to read minds. We learned to make good guesses rather than asking so many questions.

So for me and for people like me, it feels rude to ask a lot of questions. For us, it feels rude to ask someone if you can stay in their home without an invitation first. For us, it feels rude to ask someone to help you move from your apartment. For guessers like me, it may even be rude to ask someone for help with a project for work. Guessers feel like questions are inconveniences and, even worse, questions put the other person in an awkward position. *What if I ask him to help me move and he struggles to tell me no? What if I ask her if I can use her spare bedroom and she feels uncomfortable with the request? Am I putting her in an awkward position?*

Meanwhile, askers feel like it's rude when people drop hints, winks, and nods to get their needs met. Askers would argue, "If you need something, just ask me! Be direct about it. The worst thing that can happen is I'll say no."

None of this is a problem as long as guessers hang out with guessers and askers hang out with askers. Problems arise when a guesser meets an asker. *Yikes.*

Even though I'm a guesser, throughout this book, I'm going to ask you to be a bit of both if you can. When you see someone crying in the corner, I think it's fair to guess that the person is sad. You might be right. But by asking, you might find out that the person is actually scared, not sad. So maybe we can approach people with a guess-ask combo. It might sound like this: "I noticed you're sitting by yourself over here and you look kind of sad. Did I get that right?"

Guessing gives you a chance to show a person that you understand without burdening them to explain it to you. And asking gives them a chance to correct you, if your guess is wrong. When my friend was diagnosed with cancer, people kept asking her, "What do you need?" She was so annoyed because she didn't know the answer. It might have helped if people had tried the guess-ask combo. Like, "I'm guessing it's tough to manage all of your medical appointments while raising two little kids. I'd like to come by and take them to the park while you focus on your care. Would that be okay? If so, which day?"

Here are some other examples of how the guess-ask combo could appear in everyday life:

- "I'm guessing that you want to be alone, but if I'm wrong, call my cell phone. I'm free between 5:00 p.m. and 8:00 p.m. to talk."

- "I'm guessing it might be helpful if I watch the kids for you later. I intend to swing by around 7:00 p.m. with some movies and popcorn. If that's not helpful, when would be a better time?"
- "I'm guessing by your silence that you are mad at me. If I'm wrong, can you help me understand what's going on for you? I'm worried."

I can't tell you how your teenager likes to be helped. I can't tell you how your spouse likes to be helped. This book is not an attempt at mind reading. Instead, I'm going to share some tools that have some scientific evidence to support their effectiveness. I'm going to encourage you to try them out if you're willing. But at the end of the day, it will be up to you to apply these tools to scenarios in your life. You might feel like you're guessing about when a tool could be helpful. Rather than pure guessing, try the guess-ask combo.

When I am speaking to large audiences about communication skills, they often seek my approval for their sentences and questions.

- *Dr. Watson, is it okay if I ask my daughter if she and her boyfriend are practicing safe sex?*
- *Dr. Watson, is it all right if I tell my patient she needs to lose weight? And is it okay to use words like "fat" and "obese"?*
- *Dr. Watson, is it okay if I push my students to work harder? Will they feel empowered, or will they feel ashamed?*

I have no business answering those questions. I, like you, cannot read minds. The only person who can tell the nervous mother in my audience how to communicate with her daughter is her daughter. The only person who can tell the doctor how to speak to patients is the patient sitting in the exam room. The only person who can tell the teacher how to motivate a student is the student sitting in the classroom. So what do I tell people who ask me these questions? I tell them to make a thoughtful guess about how to help people and then pay close attention to the response. If the person responds well, you're probably doing something good. If the person doesn't respond well, ask them what would be more helpful. Guess and then ask. Guess and then ask.

It might sound like this: "I'm not doing a very good job of guessing what you need, so I'm just going to ask. What can I do to be helpful right now?"

Folks, you can't read minds, but you can guess and ask.

Standard #4: Embrace Vulnerability

Our world owes a debt of gratitude to Dr. Brené Brown for her massive body of work studying the role of vulnerability in our lives. The thread that connects all of Brown's books (there are six of them now) is that humans have a tendency to armor up and protect themselves from shame, pain, and failure. We spend our lives guarding against the things that may be scary or uncomfortable rather than disarming ourselves and living wholehearted and authentic lives full of mistakes and flaws.

This tendency to look away from anything ugly or uneasy creates a barrier for helpers because being helpful often means sitting in a tough, emotional place with someone. It means showing up for them when they are disgusted, disgraced, and degraded. Helpful people prove that they can sit with discomfort, even if it means enduring tears, screams, or criticisms. That is what it means to be vulnerable. You let down your guard, and you bear witness to the shit that people are dealing with.

Throughout this book, we will apply these standards of helpfulness to all kinds of common scenarios related to humor, apologies, encouragement, advice, etc. And while we take this journey together, keep in mind that I'm assuming the folks reading this book are well-intentioned helpers. I try not to waste space in the book discussing examples of times when people are acting out of malice, jealousy, hate, or a desire to control and manipulate. That shit is for another book on another day (and probably by another author). Still, I seem to get a lot of questions in my e-mail inbox like these:

- *What about my passive-aggressive roommate who purposely leaves out the peanut butter to bug me?*
- *How do I respond to my boss who is creating a toxic work environment?*
- *Why does my mother-in-law purposely try to humiliate me in front of my kids?*

These questions are impossible to answer. Look, I'm the "only trying to help" lady—not the expert on mean people. I don't even know a lot of mean people, to be honest with you. Most of my friends are teachers, doctors, nurses, social workers, and community activists. They live and breathe their visions for a better world, and I effing love them for it. But hey, they also fall on their faces a lot, and I love them for that too. So I've spent my career helping people whose hearts are already good. I just arm them with tools to channel their heart's desire. I will leave the mean ones to someone else. I know how to stay in my lane.

In my work, I often teach therapists and social workers the difference between compassion and empathy. Compassion is caring about people enough to want to help them. Empathy is your ability to understand what people may need. Ideally, we would all be very strong in compassion and empathy, but this book is written for the people who are already very good at compassion—they already care so much about other people, but they struggle with understanding what people need from a helper. When I pitched this idea to a publisher, she said, "Oh, I get it. Big hearts, low skill. That's everyone I know." Me too, sister. Me too.

Chapter 1:

Well-Meaning Encouragement

No one reaches out to you for compassion or empathy so that you can teach them how to behave better. They reach out because they believe in our capacity to sit in the dark with them. Unfortunately, we have a tendency to try to flip on the lights.
—Brené Brown, The Power of Vulnerability

Before I could legally purchase alcohol, I worked at an inpatient psychiatric hospital on a unit dedicated to the treatment of adolescent boys in crisis. Approximately twenty boys between the ages of twelve and eighteen received care for things like depression, psychosis, defiant behavior, and suicidal ideation.

The hospital's exterior was straight out of a scary movie, and of course, rumors of ghost sightings flooded the place, making the night shift spooky, to say the least. Inside, the hospital layout was surprisingly modern, bright, and even a little peaceful, despite the traumatic turmoil patients brought into the space.

Given the emotionally demanding work we did there and the unimaginable pain the mental health patients suffered, it feels slightly inappropriate to admit that I loved my job there. The staff made arduous work feel fun. Most of the time, I felt more like a camp counselor than a mental health professional. A few times a week, I escorted the higher-functioning kids to the basketball court to shoot hoops. Sometimes we watched movies, played cards, and competed in push-up challenges. Maybe it's because I never had brothers, but it was cool for me to discover that I could hang with the boys—or at least I could until they started farting and spitting. I drew the line there.

And sure, some days left the staff feeling hopeless and drained. We witnessed hard things. On my very first day of work, a married couple abandoned their twelve-year-old boy at the door of the admissions department. They basically said to him, "We can't deal with you anymore. Have a nice life." He came into the hospital with only a trash bag of dirty clothes. It was my job to sort through the bag to make sure he wasn't bringing in any restricted items: sharp objects, drugs, etc. All I found was dirty clothing and thirty-five cents of loose change at the very bottom of the bag. I cried in the laundry room where no one could see me. *What would his life have in store for him? Does he know the feeling of love at all? Did he ever know love? Would he go to school? Would he have a family someday?* I either couldn't imagine the answers to those questions or didn't want to.

I met so many kids like him over the next couple of years. They dealt with drug-addicted parents, community violence, depression, psychosis, trauma, racism, poverty, and all sorts of other heavy shit on top of just being a teenager.

It was at times dangerous work in the hospital. In my two years as an employee, I was bitten, nearly strangled, and spat on repeatedly, but despite that, I managed to find joy in my work. I think I might have worked there forever if it had paid a living wage.

I remember a two-week period when we had a patient named Marcus on the unit. We attributed his admission to the hospital to explosive oppositional behavior at school, aggression toward his peers, and a series of violent actions toward cats. But Marcus pulled on my heartstrings. He seemed so gentle and mild to me. He was short and probably a little underweight for his age. Looking at him with his skinny legs and straggly hair, I found it hard to imagine that he was the same kid who was threatening and hurting others at home and at school. Marcus struck me as a sensitive soul with a kind heart.

We would make up stories together. I'd begin with a character: *Let's start the story with a king. Now you go, Marcus!*

He would build the story and then pass it back to me: *Um . . . the king is really sad, and he wants to move away from his kingdom. Now you go, Miss Kate!*

I would try to add a twist to make him laugh: *So the king moves to Florida, and now he scoops ice cream at Disney World. Your turn, Marcus!*

I'm never sure how much to trust my own memory, but when I think about those days, I recall our stories lasting hours and hours, but I guess that couldn't have been true. The hospital program maintained a strict schedule, and the stories maybe lasted twenty minutes at most because we didn't have that much downtime. Regardless, the storytelling was fun, and it helped us build a relationship.

The kids on our unit, for the most part, had been kicked out of the public school system, abandoned by their families, and failed by the child welfare system. Yet it was easy to forget all that when we could just play together.

As would take place at any hospital, we received a lengthy shift change report on arrival. The charge nurse from the morning shift would audio record a summary of the day's happenings, including a report on every patient in the unit. The afternoon shift arrived at 3:00 p.m. to hear the report, and in theory, they'd be ready to take over responsibilities of the unit by 3:30 p.m. when the morning shift clocked out.

One particular day, I came in for my evening shift and sat down with my afternoon coffee and listened to the report. I learned that some boys on the unit had tirelessly teased Marcus and called him "pussy boy" because of his behavior with cats. A fight broke out, and it was Marcus versus three or four older and bigger boys. Fortunately, the staff got everything under control, and no one was seriously injured—not physically, anyway. But Marcus was embarrassed, scared, and overwhelmed by the whole experience.

According to the nurse's report, he had secluded himself in his room for the bulk of the day.

When the report was over, I volunteered to check on him. I can remember so clearly how it felt to be traipsing down that very sterile and clinical hallway, thinking, *Being a kid is so damn hard. I wish I could make things easier for him.*

I nervously tapped on his door and announced myself. "Hey, Marcus. It's Miss Kate. How's it going, buddy?" There was no answer. I walked in and said, "Hey, you . . . I heard you had a rough day. It's not too late to turn it around. Are we going to have fun tonight? I will let you pick the movie later. You down?"

Marcus said, "I have no friends, and everybody hates me. My parents won't let me have a birthday party because they think no one will come!" My eyes filled with tears as I listened, and I felt my throat constrict. I thought, *What a life he's led already by age twelve.*

I stood next to his bed, feeling aghast and inarticulate, but in an act of desperation, I said, "Look, Marcus, it's going to be okay." His head was still buried in a pillow, and I repeated, "Come on, look at me. It's gonna be okay. Do you hear me?" Marcus rolled over, his face beet red and soaked in tears.

"Please leave me alone! Puh-lease!"

I am from Philadelphia, so naturally, I channeled my best Rocky Balboa attitude and got ready to launch into "It ain't how hard you get hit..." I instead settled for "Come on, bud. I heard what happened. It's no biggie. Everyone is going to forget about this by tomorrow. They've moved on to something else by now. You hear me? It's over. It's squashed."

Marcus said, "Fine. Can you go now, please?"

"Don't get snappy with me, Marcus. You want to know something? I've been through this too, believe it or not. I really do get it. I've been teased. I used to get picked on for being an overweight kid. It sucks, but we all go through it. Look, I survived, and you will too. It's character building, you know? You'll be stronger than them in the end. Look at it that way."

He placated me, just as I had been placating him. "Okay, whatever."

"You think you're the first person to get picked on? Puh-lease! I didn't let it get me down. I just ignored them and moved on."

"Miss Kate, they did it in front of everyone!"

"I understand, but you just need to stop worrying about what people think. Stay above it. You're too good for all this childish nonsense that they're up to."

He pleaded with me, "Can you please leave me alone now?"

But I was relentless. "No, come to the group room with me. We're getting ready to watch a movie soon. I will let you pick it out. Let's go. Save your tears for something important, okay?"

"Maybe later. I'm just gonna hang here for now. I'm fine though. Really. It's fine."

We so often do this to children. We view their grumpy moods, bad days, and bad attitudes as problems for us to solve rather than accept the human experience. Frankly, society allows adults to have more bad days than children can have. We act like their humanity is dysfunctional, holding them to a higher standard than we hold ourselves, and we do this because it's difficult to witness their anguish without desperately trying to save them from it.

Even if you don't have children, you know the agony of watching another person suffer. We don't want people to feel as hurt as we have felt, so we encourage them to feel better or to think positively. As helpers though, we should act more like supportive partners than protectors or peacemakers. Although I may have thought my actions were for Marcus's benefit, much of my behavior served to ease my own agony. I was uncomfortable with his pain, and I wanted to feel better. I so badly needed to see that happy, gentle kid again. By encouraging him to be happy, I was trying to meet my own needs, not his.

When I look back on that conversation with Marcus, I'd prefer to blame my behavior on the fact that I was really young and inexperienced and I had not yet been trained as a therapist. But the truth is, I still sometimes behave the same way, and I've been in this field now for fifteen years. Not too long ago, my good friend called me and told me she thought her boyfriend was cheating on her. Feeling ill equipped to help her, eager to do something useful, and like a fraud as a helping professional, I did the easiest, the most obvious, and frankly, the laziest thing I could do: I reassured her that everything would be fine (which is a lie), encouraged her to just keep doing what she's doing (which is potentially a bad idea), and advised her to go with her gut (which is super unhelpful and vague).

When I finished distinguishing her with all my meaningless platitudes, she responded by saying, "Thanks. How's your job going, by the way? Sorry, I didn't even ask." She changed the subject. She gave up on me as a helper, and I can't blame her. My attempt to encourage her left me feeling like such a waste of space.

As usual, my heart was in the right place when I offered her encouragement, but like all good things, encouragement has its limits. In this chapter, we will explore the times that well-meaning encouragement may backfire or potentially cause more harm than good, as was the case with the friend who called and also in my experience with Marcus.

Let's see what else we can learn by running through our four standards.

Standard #1: Listen More Than You Speak

In my example of working with Marcus, I stopped listening to him so I could insert my own ideas about what he should do. I tried to pump him up and make him see my perspective rather than understand his. I spoke to him, and when my words didn't help, I spoke more. When that didn't help, I spoke more again. I wasn't listening, and Marcus knew it. He knew I wasn't interested in understanding, only fixing.

When we encourage people to think positively or to persevere in some way, we are essentially attempting to change their feelings, which is impossible to do on demand. Instead, it's more helpful to speak with empathy, which is our ability to understand and accept how a person feels without attempting to fix or change it. Empathy is merely the act of saying "I hear you" or "I see you." Empathy is not reassurance. I tried, for example, to reassure Marcus by saying, "It's going to be okay." But showing empathy sounds more like this: "I see that you're feeling embarrassed and lonely."

If I had shown more empathy, I would have proven to Marcus that he was free to be himself with me. I would have proven to him I was brave enough to sit with him through some yucky feelings. He may have even felt comfortable telling me more. He might have thought to himself, *She really gets it*. To feel understood is among the greatest feelings in the world. We mean well when we encourage people to be positive, but empathy is the way to go.

Emotional empathy reveals our ability to understand the feelings that a person conveys with their words, tone, and body language. This may require you to develop a more robust emotional vocabulary than you're used to accessing (see Appendix C). For example, rather than saying to someone "That must be really hard," maybe you could name a specific emotion: "That must leave you feeling betrayed" or "I bet you're feeling discouraged." Often you'll find that people feel relieved to have a word to describe their experience, and they will gleefully exclaim, "Yes! That's what I'm trying to say!"

Think back to elementary school. When you completed math problems, you were not allowed to just fill in the answer. You had to show your work, right? The teacher wanted to see that you understood the math on a deeper level. Expressions of empathy are no different. You can't get away with just saying things like "I get it" or "I understand." Instead, you show

how you got there. Here are some examples of showing your work with empathic statements:

Person A	Response from Person B Example of "showing your work"
I can't believe my friends didn't stick up for me.	You feel betrayed.
I'm really putting off talking to my kids about the divorce.	You're feeling anxious about it.
Can you believe my boss canceled the meeting again?	You're tired of feeling rejected.

Every year, I speak to thousands of people about empathy. Whether I'm speaking to doctors, teachers, social workers, or police officers, one of the most common questions I get is "How is it helpful to say back to someone what they just said to me? I feel like I'm not doing anything." Folks, we drastically overestimate the power we have over the quality of another person's feelings, and we underestimate the power of just understanding how they feel right now. In a 2013 (Miller & Moyers) study called "Is Low Therapist Empathy Toxic?" researchers found that when therapists used empathic statements to show both cognitive and emotional understanding, clients who screened positively for alcohol abuse were more likely to reduce their alcohol consumption. The more surprising result was that the control group—those who received no treatment at all—were better off than participants who worked with a therapist who struggled with expressing empathy. This means that people are better off on their own than they are relying on a helper who is empathy deficient.

How can that be true? Well, understanding a person's feelings can help you understand the messages they cannot articulate. Is the person showing aggression, for example? Maybe the person feels threatened. Is the person expressing jealous feelings? Maybe this person isn't who they aspire to be. Is the person exuding joy? Then maybe the moment has deep meaning for the person. Is the person showing fear? Then maybe the person needs more safety. Often, when it's anger, it means the person is trying to protect or defend something. Whatever the case may be, the point is that naming feelings can tell you a lot about the person's needs. But to name the feelings, you have to be willing to sit with them—even the tough ones. You may, at times, doubt that your heart can take it. Try anyway. Zelda Fitzgerald said, "No one has ever measured, not even poets, how much the heart can hold." So, folks, I say give your heart a chance to shine.

Standard #2: Assert and Respect Boundaries

As a reminder, boundaries separate what belongs to me from what belongs to you. I worry that when we engage in well-meaning encouragement, we also take responsibility for feelings and attitudes that are not our own to manage. Let me give you some examples of this. As a public speaker, I get a lot of audience questions about how to fix other people's feelings. Check them out:

- Dr. Watson, how do I make my teenage daughter feel better after she was bullied at school?

- Dr. Watson, how can I make my husband feel better now that he has been rejected for a promotion?

- Dr. Watson, how should I make my friend feel better after her cancer diagnosis? I want to cheer her up.

I say the same thing to all of them: *You're missing the point. Stop trying to encourage people to feel happy, grateful, accepting, or excited. You have no control over that. It's beyond your boundaries, and it's a violation of the boundaries to which your loved ones are entitled. No amount of encouragement is going to make a person's pain go away.*

I'm never less mad because someone told me, "Don't be mad. Look on the bright side." I'm never less scared because someone told me, "Don't worry. Everything is going to be okay." Feelings just don't work that way. So it's important to set a boundary to establish what you can and cannot control.

I like to explain it to my clients this way: We all have emotional "tanks" (like fish tanks) that fill up and empty throughout the day. I have an anger tank that holds my anger. On bad days, my anger tank gets pretty full, and I need to empty some anger out by practicing a coping skill like deep breathing, talking a walk, or screaming into a pillow. I have an excited tank that holds my excitement. Right before vacations and holidays, my excitement tank gets pretty full, and I start showing it everywhere I go. I say things like "I just cannot contain my excitement!" When someone compliments my work, I feel my pride tank fill up a bit. When I see a person who lives on the street, I feel my sad tank fill up a bit. When my neighbors are blasting their music so loud that I can't hear my TV, I feel my annoyed tank fill up a lot! I have an embarrassed tank, a nervous tank, a joyous tank, and hundreds of others. All day long, I can feel my tanks filling up or emptying. That's how feelings work, and emotionally intelligent people notice their tank levels all throughout the day.

Respecting a person's emotional boundaries is just fancy talk for leaving your hands off another person's tank. When my colleague is angry, there is nothing I can do about that. Only he controls his tank. When my best friend is disappointed, there is nothing I can do about that either. She controls her tank. I have to let the people in my life have their feelings. That is their right. To respect boundaries means staying on my side of the line and not saying things like "Don't feel bad" or "Don't get upset." When I say those things, I'm trying to manage another person's tank, and that's impossible to do.

The best thing you can do is help the person identify which tank is in trouble. You might say something like "I get the sense that you're feeling defeated, and you need to let that out right now." You might even try the tank analogy, if you're brave. You could say something like "I wonder if your loneliness tank is calling out for a little help right now."

To encourage a person to feel differently is like judging what fills their tank. Unfortunately, I was guilty of that when I worked with Marcus.

In my own way, I told him that the bullying he experienced was silly and that he shouldn't be upset. I was judging what filled up his tank. Then I tried to empty his tank with well-meaning efforts at encouragement. I tried to cheer him up, and I failed. So let me be loud and clear—don't judge what fills a person's tank and don't manage another person's tank.

Any attempt to "fix" somebody is shameful because it implies the person is broken. A more helpful approach is to see them for who they are today and to value them in whatever state that is: happy, sad, scared, angry, or defeated. Send the message that all are welcome here. Come as you are.

I practice this concept with a little kid I know. In the past, when he would explode in anger because I didn't buy him a toy, I used to judge him for that. I'd say, "You should be grateful. Some kids have no toys at all!" But I've learned that when his anger tank is full, it's full. It's up to him to open the valve and release the emotion until his tank is back to a tolerable level. So now I thank him for letting me know he is mad. He still isn't getting the toy, but he can be angry. I mean, realistically, his anger exists regardless of my approval. That's what it means to hold boundaries. His tank is his tank. I can't encourage him or his tank to cheer up.

Let go of the control you imagine yourself to have. You never had it to begin with. You can't change a person's feelings. Instead, show them how brave you are to feel right along with them.

In 2016, when Donald Trump shocked the world by winning the Electoral College in the U.S. presidential election, I, like so many others, felt stunned. My dad sent me a text message saying, "I know you must be so disappointed. If you want, we can meet for coffee, and you can just vent or yell or scream or whatever." I don't know how he voted—that's not the point, and it's none of my business. The point is that he could have called and analyzed how the Clinton campaign didn't focus enough on the Rust Belt states. He could have tried to make me laugh by joking about Trump's obvious stupidity. He could have reassured me that politics is always messy, and this year is just like all the others. But he did none of those things, and

I love him for it. He didn't try to change my feelings at all. He offered some space for my feelings to exist. He was just going to let me be effing mad. He didn't try to fix my tank, but he was willing to sit with me while I emptied it out myself. Man, I bet he was a great bartender back in the 1980s.

Standard #3: Forgive Yourself for Not Reading Minds

The theme running throughout this chapter is "Don't rely on encouragement to support people when all you need to do is show that you understand and accept them." But understanding people can be difficult, and I'm not asking you to read minds. Just do your best.

Admittedly, the skill of empathic listening requires you to take some guesses about how a person feels. It's like a little leap of faith. Check out these examples:

Remark from Person A	Person B's "Guess" or "Small Leap" of Understanding
I can't wait for this weekend.	*You have so much to look forward to this weekend.* (This is a small leap because it is not exactly what Person A said.)
I'm nervous about my test tomorrow.	*You have invested a lot in this exam, and it's tough to perform under all that stress.* (This is a small leap because it is not exactly what Person A said.)
What if I tell my boyfriend that I love him and he doesn't say it back?	*You're worried about putting your heart on the line.* (This is a small leap because it is not exactly what Person A said.)

I recommend that you only leap as far as you trust the other person to bring you back if you've gone too far. The stronger the relationship, the farther you can leap. With a person you love and with whom you have a deep, trusting relationship, it is not too risky to take a big leap because that person is far more likely to correct you and bring you back to reality. If, however, you're trying this skill with someone you've just met, leap with extreme caution. You can't be sure that person will correct you, so take tiny leaps and express empathy more conservatively.

Only Trying to Help started as a podcast I hosted with my good friend Leslie. I asked her to join me for the podcast because she's smart, funny, and really well-spoken. Above all else, she's a friend I trust. While I wrote this book, Leslie surprised me with an unexpected phone call—unexpected especially since we share an aversion to speaking on the phone.

I answered and said, "Hey, what's up, lady?"

She blurted out in a mix of tears and gasping for air, "My mom died."

I thought to myself, *Oh shit, I need to really show up for her right now.* I felt scared that I might let Leslie down. I said, "Okay, I'm just going to sit down for a second. I know I'm being quiet over here, but I'm just absorbing this."

For about a minute—a *real* minute—no one spoke, except for the occasional F-bomb. We just listened to each other cry into the phone.

And then I said, "I'm glad you called me, Leslie. You shouldn't go through this alone."

And then we were quiet again. I'm not sure for how long.

Eventually, Leslie broke the silence and gushed, "She was my best friend. There was no one better. There will never be anyone better. She was my everything. If I needed anything, I called her. She was always there for me. I don't know what I'm going to do. I will never be the same. She was perfect, Kate. She was perfect. I'm here in the house, looking at her perfect things. What am I going to do, Kate? She was my best friend. I will never be the same. People don't even know, but she was amazing. She was everything. She was everything."

I let Leslie hear me take a deep inhale and a deep exhale. It was purposeful. I wanted her to know that I was going slow, that I was taking my time, and that I could hold her pain without it sending me into a fit of anxiety. I wanted her to hear the rhythm of my calming breath.

I said, "For you right now, the ground feels rocky. She was a part of you."

She seemed to elaborate. "Everything is on me now, and I don't know what to do."

I said, "Life feels uncertain, and you were not prepared for all this responsibility."

She talked about other people in her life who had died and how, even though it was painful, she was largely prepared for their deaths. They had been sick, and it was well-known that the end was near. Her mom, however, was perfectly healthy and suddenly suffered a heart attack.

I said, "Even though we're never fully prepared for death, this was extraordinarily unexpected. It's like the rug has been pulled out from under you."

Leslie and I stayed on the phone for an hour. We mostly cried and took deep breaths. Deep inhale, deep exhale. Repeat.

Folks, I've never lost a parent. I don't know what it feels like to lose a mom or a dad. I didn't even try to claim that I understood. In this case, Leslie and I weren't sharing the same experience, but we could connect on familiar feelings. I haven't lost my parents, but I have felt grief. I haven't lost my parents, but I have felt uncertainty. I haven't lost my parents, but I have felt beat up by an unwelcome surprise. Connect on feelings, not experiences. Your experiences will always be different from another person's, but to be human is to connect with the feelings of the people around you.

I didn't offer Leslie pitiful platitudes like "She's in a better place" or "Everything happens for a reason." I made no attempts to make Leslie feel better. I didn't encourage her to heal or be positive. I only tried to understand her, all the while knowing my limits at how well I could understand. I reflected back my understanding with statements like

- *"For you right now, the ground feels rocky. She was a part of you."*

- *"Life feels uncertain, and you were not prepared for all this responsibility."*
- *"It's like the rug has been pulled out from under you."*

I took a small leap to guess her feelings, and I could have been wrong. That's not a crime. Sometimes you'll take a guess at how a person feels, and they will respond with "Well, no, not really. That's not what I'm trying to say." No need for alarm. This is common.

In this kind of scenario, I like to imagine a dartboard. The bull's-eye represents the exact thing the person is trying to convey. When you speak empathic statements, it's like you're throwing darts and you're trying to get as close as possible to the bull's-eye. The key is forgiving yourself for never hitting dead center. You'd have to live the other person's life to hit dead center. It's impossible. Your only goal is to get as close as possible.

Standard #4: Embrace Vulnerability

Very often, people will lean on encouragement as a tool when they themselves feel uncomfortable with vulnerability. I want to tip my hat to American television icon Mr. Fred Rogers, who so eloquently exposed this phenomenon. He remarked, "People have said, 'Don't cry,' to other people for years and years, and all it has ever meant is 'I'm too uncomfortable when you show your feelings.' I'd rather have them say, 'Go ahead and cry. I'm here to be with you.'"

Mr. Rogers is a damn genius. Personally, I don't want someone to come along to fix me or my mood. I want someone to stick with me while I fix myself. I want someone to witness my marathon of anguish and watch in awe while I conquer every hurdle in my way. When I'm struggling, don't you dare think, *I need to encourage her to feel better*. Instead, please think to yourself, *I'm not going anywhere. I'm going to stay here and watch her survive, and that shit is going to be stunning.*

My best friend Julie once said to me, "Oh, this year is going to be hell for you, Kate. It really is. But you will not walk through hell alone. I got you, sister. Ride or die." That's a goddamn friend. If you don't have that friend, find that friend because you *deserve* that friend.

Let go of this myth that we can change a person's feelings with encouragement or reassurance. Your words will sound nice, but the message they convey is either "You shouldn't feel that way" or "I'm uncomfortable when you feel that way" or both. It's more helpful to show your strength for tolerating their pain. Say "I can handle this" instead of "Don't be sad." Show you are brave enough to tolerate the crappy feelings. Prove that you have the guts.

I have a friend who likes to call me on his bad days. He says, "Hey, I'm just calling because I've had a horrible day and I'm really angry right now."

My response: "Anger? Okay. We can handle that. Let's be angry. What are we angry about?"

"I'm just so stressed right now, and I feel like I'm going crazy, and I just needed to talk it out."

"Stress? That's a familiar one. Let's stress together. What's stressing you right now?"

That is emotional grit. He knows that his feelings (even the ugly ones) are welcome in my world and I'm not afraid of them.

Unfortunately, people are so uncomfortable with difficult feelings like anger, sadness, anxiety, and guilt that they chronically put a positive spin on things. Recently, this tendency to push for positive feelings has been coined *toxic positivity*. It sounds like these:

- "Just keep going!"
- "Let it go!"
- "Don't think about it that way."
- "Don't get mad. It's no big deal."
- "Don't be scared. It's going to be okay."

- "Don't worry. You'll do a great job!"
- "Don't get nervous. You'll crush it!"
- "Don't be negative. Look on the bright side."

These statements are well-meaning attempts at encouragement, but they are impatient, insincere, and dismissive. These statements come from a person's immature need to feel comfortable rather than a person's vulnerability. I propose we offer people empathy, validation, and hope instead. It sounds like these:

- "You're about to do a really difficult thing (empathy). It makes perfect sense to be nervous about it (validation). I'm not sure if it makes any difference, but I'm really confident you can do this despite your nerves (hope)."
- "This sucks (empathy). It's normal to have some negativity in this kind of situation (validation). I'm perfectly comfortable with you showing your genuine feelings so I can help you through it at your own pace (hope)."
- "You're not feeling confident about this (empathy). I get that (validation). I know I can't change how you feel, and we can make sense of it later (hope)."
- "It's always so hard (validation) when the shit hits the fan (empathy). Is there something we can do today that you might enjoy . . . even a little? (hope)."

But unfortunately, people lack awareness of their toxic positivity. I learned this hard truth in 2017 when I ran a marathon. First, let me say I will never run a marathon again. I will not run a marathon for a new car, and I will not run a marathon for a million dollars. I sure *as hell* will not run a marathon to beat my personal record or some other competitive shit like that.

When I ran my marathon, I suffered. I cried for the final seven miles of the race, which, as it turns out, is a great way to dehydrate yourself during a marathon. I looked as miserable as I felt.

All over the racecourse, supporters cheered us on, yelling things like "You go, girl!" and "You got this!" and even when I had six miles left to go, they'd yell bullshit like "You're almost there!" Eff you. No, I'm not. "You're doing great!" Eff you. No, I'm not. "You look fantastic!" Eff you. No, I don't. Well-meaning encouragement and toxic positivity was running ramped (pun intended).

Of course, not everyone at the race suffered from toxic positivity. While I limped my way to mile twenty-two or twenty-three, a woman who looked like a young Carly Simon locked eyes with me from the cheering section. She lifted out of her cushy chair, put down her ice-cold beer (God, love her for that), stepped on to the marathon course, and started jogging next to me. She half smiled at me the way people do when they're nervous to ask a question. Then she compassionately and kindly said, "You seem like you're in pain. Do you need anything?"

I had salty tears dripping off my chin and no energy to speak, so I just moved my head side to side to indicate no. Then she said, still jogging next to me, "I know this is absolutely miserable, but you've conquered twenty-two miles already. I don't know too many people who have done that. And even if you crawl across the finish line, you will make it. For now, it's time to just manage the pain."

This time I nodded in agreement. I mean, I really wanted to embrace her, thank her, and declare her my new best friend, but I was barely standing upright, so I whispered out a "thanks," and she peeled off the course, returning to her seat. She validated my pain, and she gave me hope I could survive, but she didn't ask me to look good or smile or feel happy at all. She let me finish my misery. She's a saint.

It's not that hope and optimism are bad. They are not bad, but they are also not sufficient. They do not stand on their own very well. There is a difference between saying "You're going to be fine! You always are!" and "I have no doubt that you'll be fine because you always are. I also know that your spirit is heavy right now, and I don't want you to hide that from me. Your heavy spirit is welcome here. I can handle it."

This makes me think of a time when I was riding in a taxi in my hometown of Philadelphia. I was on my way to a meeting with my dissertation advisor, and I was nervous to the point of nausea. I had spent the morning practicing coping skills to calm my anxiety, but nothing seemed to help. The taxi driver noticed my quiet and intense focus, so he asked, "You good, girl?"

I told him I was feeling uneasy about a big meeting. He casually said, "Yeah you got that stomach flip. Am I right?" I nodded and then told him about my meeting.

As he pulled up to the university, and I opened the door to exit, he stopped me. He said, "Hey, I know you're nervous. This is a hard thing to do. I know you don't want to hear this right now, but you're going to be fine. You're a smart woman, and that's gonna take you far, girl."

Folks, didn't I tell you that counselors appear where you least expect them? And I don't mean to imply any surprise that a taxi driver was capable of such empathy and vulnerability. In fact, I was more surprised that a man—no matter his profession, was so emotionally intelligent. Perhaps no one is as limited in this area as men, who are taught some rather unrelenting messages about vulnerability throughout their lives: *Do not appear to be weak. Do not express yourself in any way that might break the rules. Be tall. Be strong. Be productive. Be stoic. Make money.* All you have to do is scan a men's clothing store with your eyes to see how we have limited men's ability to express themselves: Every item of clothing is blue, gray, and black. Have you ever looked at a store catalog or website under the section "gifts for him"? Your options are flasks, knives, and neckties. What's the message? Men can go to work (wearing the necktie), numb their feelings (with the flask), and destroy things (with the knife). The section for women includes art, gardening, and self-care products. So women are allowed to create things, grow things, and entice their senses with smells and sounds.

Maybe no one described this better than feminist author bell hooks (2004), who wrote, "The first act of violence that patriarchy demands of males is not violence toward women. Instead, patriarchy demands of all males that they engage in acts of psychic self-mutilation, that they kill off the emotional parts of themselves. If an individual is not successful in emotionally crippling himself, he can count on patriarchal men to enact rituals of power that will assault his self-esteem."

Brené Brown wrote about this phenomenon in her book *Daring Greatly*. I will never forget reading about her interview with a man who said, "My wife and daughters—the ones you signed all of those books for—they'd rather see me die on top of my white horse than watch me fall off." Brown used *The Wizard of Oz* to make sense of her interviews with men. She said,

> Over the past couple of years, especially since the economic downturn, what I have started to see is the box from *The Wizard of Oz*. I'm talking about the small, curtain-concealed box that the wizard stands in as he's controlling his mechanical "great and powerful" Oz image. As scarcity has grabbed hold of our culture, it's not just "don't be perceived as weak" but also "you better be great and all powerful." This image first came to mind when I interviewed a man who was in deep shame about getting downsized. He told me, "It's funny. My father knows. My two closest friends know. But my wife doesn't know. It's been six months, and every morning I still get dressed and leave the house like I'm going to work. I drive across town, sit in coffee shops, and look for a job."
>
> I'm a skilled interviewer, but I can imagine that the look on my face conveyed something like, "How on earth did you pull that

off?" Without waiting for my next questions, he answered, "She doesn't want to know. If she already knows, she wants me to keep pretending. Trust me, if I find another job, and tell her after I'm back to work, she'll be grateful. Knowing would change the way she feels about me. She didn't sign up for this."

I was not prepared to hear over and over from men how the women—the mothers, sisters, girlfriends, wives—in their lives are constantly criticizing them for not being open and vulnerable and intimate, all the while they are standing in front of that cramped wizard closet where their men are huddled inside, adjusting the curtain and making sure no one sees in and no one gets out. There was a moment when I was driving home from an interview with a small group of men and thought, Holy Shit. I am the patriarchy.

Folks, don't encourage anyone's feelings away. Male, female, young, old, black, white, we all feel a lot of ugly shit. That's how we recognize the happier days. We can't really know joy until we've known pain. We can't really know pride until we've known shame. Help your friends, family, and colleagues feel a full range of human emotions because it creates a fuller life. By telling them to cheer up, be positive, and look on the bright side, we kill off their emotional selves, little by little.

Chapter 2:
Well-Meaning Compliments

"So long as men praise you, you can only be sure that you are not yet on your own path, but on someone else's."
—Friedrich Nietzsche

I serve as a consultant to a nonprofit organization that provides counseling services to domestic violence survivors in the United States. Part of my role is to advise the board of directors and to help inform some of their clinical decision-making and strategic plans for the organization.

It's not all hard work though. We have fun too. They have the meetings catered, they bring in guest speakers with engaging presentations, and sometimes there is a social hour with music, networking, and when we are lucky, a glass of wine.

One member, nicknamed Santa Claus for his folksy and friendly demeanor, once threw his arms around my waist and said, "What's your secret, girl? You're really slimming down!" The way he poked my side made me want to bathe in Purell immediately. A smirk temporarily colonized my face, and I said, "Just taking good care of myself," before I quickly changed the subject away from my physical appearance.

In a recent meeting with this group and some of its key stakeholders, I introduced myself to the room, sharing a brief biography, just like everyone else had done. Santa Claus interrupted me to ask, "Gosh! How old are you?" I turned red and fell speechless. He realized the embarrassment he caused, but he expressed no remorse. Instead, he pointed at me and laughed while he said, "Look at her cheeks turning beet red! Relax, hon, you're just a really smart cookie, that's all. We're impressed with you, dear."

He wore his slimy business executive entitlement like armor against the academic elite who surrounded him.

Later, he approached me. I wasn't sure if I even wanted an apology, but I assumed I was about to get one. I was wrong. He seemed to pat me on my lower back—though it felt more like a pat on the head—when he said, "Don't worry, hon. You're doin' just fine."

Enraged, I thought to myself, *I'm doing fine? I know I'm doing fine. I'm not the one who committed a huge faux pas in the meeting. I was a professional. I was prepared. I was insightful.* Why was he trying to wipe my tears away for me when I didn't have any tears to wipe?

Years ago, I probably would have smiled, giggled, and bashfully said, "Gee thanks, Mr. So-and-so!" But I am a woman in my thirties now. I own a house. I run an international business. I have a doctorate degree. I completed a fucking marathon, for Christ's sake! I didn't need reassurance of my place in that meeting—he did.

So I said, "Right. I am doing fine. And how are you doing?"

I really don't recall his response, so I suppose it couldn't have been profound. If he had said, "I'm horribly embarrassed by my behavior, and I feel I owe you an apology," I would have remembered. So all I really know of him is his faux pas and how he made me feel small.

I can, of course, offer a generous defense of this man if I choose to. He has been taught his entire life that women should be thin, and that they want to be thin, and that it's okay to compliment them for being thin. He was trying to help in his own way. I didn't write about him in this book because he's a bad person. I dedicate this entire book to well-meaning people who sometimes put their own feet in their mouths, and I think this man could be their king. He's still a thoughtful person in his own way. It is, however, important to explore how well-meaning compliments can have a harmful impact on your relationships with people. He may have aimed to be the funny old guy in the room, but he missed the mark.

I would argue that his "compliments" like "You're a smart cookie" were microaggressions—brief remarks that send harmful messages to a vulnerable group of people. According to Dr. Derald Wing Sue, who coined the term *microaggression*, these comments can reveal biases held consciously or unconsciously. Even though they may be brief and only subtly hurtful, the impact can still be serious. This happens all around us.

I would consider it a microaggression when, in the board meeting, Santa Claus was surprised by my intelligence and experience. When he said in front of the entire conference room, "You're a smart cookie!" he had a tone of surprise in his voice. He was subtly saying, "I didn't expect that from you." To me, he was revealing his implicit bias.

So many well-meaning compliments are received as microaggressions. Look at these examples:

- A well-meaning compliment to a young girl: "Wow, you're so good at math. Did your dad or brother teach you?" This statement implies that girls lack math skills.

- A well-meaning compliment to a black student at a prestigious university: "It's awesome that you got into this school. How were you accepted?" This question implies that the student must have been accepted through a special program and couldn't have been accepted through the normal application process.

- People often praise my friend Ricky for his success. They say things like "You've come so far!" and "You're really an inspiration." He doesn't know how to respond, however, when people say things like "I can't believe how much better you've done than your family" or "Your parents must be so proud that you've been more successful than they were." It puts him in a position of comparing himself to his loved ones and potentially even feeling pitted against them. It also feels simultaneously like a compliment to him and a slight to his folks. The "compliment," if you can even call it that, implies that there is something wrong with the way he grew up.

One day, I was at work when a colleague approached and said, "You're so much more stylish than the other women around here." Again, it was simultaneously a compliment to me and a slight to my friends and colleagues. To say thank you feels like I'm joining in on the attack.

See Appendix D for more examples of microaggressions.

The goal of this chapter is not to scare people away from complimenting one another. Instead, this is a call for all of us to compliment better. In fact, to identify and name the good in others is a very helpful tool. Let's explore it through the four standards to see how Santa (yes, I'm going to keep calling him that) could have complimented me in a way I would have received better.

Standard #1: Listen More Than You Speak

Santa Claus wasn't even listening to the content and quality of my recommendations. If he had truly heard me, he would have responded with more than "You're a smart cookie." He would have commented specifically on the strengths of my proposal. Had he listened carefully, rather than trying to make himself look like the nice old grandfather in the room, he might have revealed something helpful like "Your suggestion about utilizing remote learning is exactly what our clients and staff need." If you really want to see the good in people and point it out, you're going to have to listen, and it's going to be powerful when you do. Really listening will allow you to respond with care rather than just react.

I have an anxious colleague. Sometimes she calls me and rattles off a battery of questions: "Are you traveling for work this week? How are you getting there? You're not going to be in the South, are you? I heard there is a hurricane heading for the South. Now that I think about it, I'm pretty sure you mentioned something about going to a southern state. Gosh, I sure hope you're not going to get stuck in that storm. What would you do?

I mean, you'll probably lose cell phone reception, and you won't be able to call us, so I don't know how we'll even hear from you. Do you have someone you can stay with? You might get stuck in the airport, honestly. I know you would sleep in an airport, but I wouldn't sleep in an airport. What would you do with your purse while you are sleeping? Maybe it's a town that's more inland, so you'll be okay, don't you think?"

If I reacted quickly, I might say something like "Holy Jesus, slow down and let me answer a goddamn question!" But I'm learning to respond more thoughtfully rather than merely react. So instead, I ask myself, "What is my colleague really trying to tell me?" The answer: She worries about me. Then I ask myself, "Can I find the good in that?" The answer: Sure. So when I can finally get a word in, I try to say something like "Thank you for being so considerate."

I'd be lying if I told you I'm always able to come up with that response. It's hard, and I'm a work in progress. The point is I had to listen through all the anxiety and find the message and its strength. This kind of compliment helps people. My anxious colleague calms down immediately. After I see the good in her, she slows down, and she's able to have a regular conversation with me—one where I'm allowed to participate and everything. It's important for me to refile her in my mind. She's not my "anxious colleague"; she's my "very considerate colleague."

I have even used this strategy as a college professor. I often teach in the evenings after spending the daytime hours delivering workshops and speeches for my consulting company. It's not unusual for my day to include twelve hours of public speaking between an eight-hour workshop and a four-hour night class. On one of those days, when I was completely drained, I ended class a bit early. As the students were exiting the room, I gathered up my belongings and fantasized about the large glass of wine I intended to pour myself on returning home. My fantasy was interrupted when an older student, who had an uncanny resemblance to actress Viola Davis, approached me and said, "Dr. Watson, may I ask you a question?"

I cautiously nodded while I felt my glass of wine slipping away from reality. "What's on your mind?"

She took a deep inhale, as if she was about to swim a long distance, and then exploded with rapid speech. "Well, can you help me? I don't understand how to incorporate citations into my research paper. I'm really not sure that I did the reference page correctly. Does that go in alphabetical order or chronological order? And if it's chronological, does that go by the year it was published or the order in which I used it in my paper? And can you read my introduction? I don't really understand what I'm supposed to put in there. How long should it be? Did I do that right? And am I supposed to have subtitles throughout the paper? And if so, should they be bold, or should I underline them? And do they get centered, or do they stay lined up with everything else? And then I don't understand this one article that I want to include. Can you read it and help me understand it? Also, there is another section of my paper that I think is messed up. Can you check that out too? How do I use a semicolon? And what do you think about my title? I think it's too boring. Does that matter? And also . . . um . . ."

Before Viola (that's what I like to call her now) completed her thought, she paused for some oxygen, and thank goodness she did, or she might have passed out. I seized the very brief pause to add, "Wow. You are working so hard on this paper. That's impressive." Her shoulders relaxed. She took a deep inhale and a slow exhale while she nodded. Then she said, "Thanks, I appreciate that. I will see you next week." And. She. Left.

I thought to myself, *She'll be back. I didn't answer any of her questions.* I waited. Viola didn't come back. Then I thought, *She'll e-mail me or call me.* She had about ten different ways to reach me if she wanted to. She didn't use any of them. Instead, she wrote the paper. She submitted the assignment. It was beautiful. She earned an A grade. I thought to myself, *When she asked me all those questions, it was never really about the paper. Underneath all those questions, she had a bigger, more important question.*

I can't know for sure what that question was, but I imagine it was something like "Dr. Watson, do I belong here? Am I enough?" And when I told her I was impressed with her hard work, I answered that question. In this case, I listened for her strengths and observed them aloud. I resisted the urge to spew out answers to all her questions. I could have gone on a long speech about APA formatting and developing paragraphs and integrating research, but I didn't. I listened carefully for her strengths. It saved me a lot of time and her a lot of self-doubt.

In 2015, researchers at the University of Pennsylvania (Falk, et al.) conducted a study that equipped participants with a fitness tracker to wear. They also divided the participants into two groups: intervention and control. They offered the control group information about the benefits of exercise. They offered the intervention group the same information, but before the researchers tried to educate them, the researchers first explored the strengths of each participant in the intervention group. They spoke to the participants in a way that highlighted all the noble qualities they possessed and then followed it up with information about the benefits of exercise. It may not surprise that the group who was positively affirmed ultimately exercised more than the group who only received education. That may be interesting, but that particular research finding isn't what interests me.

I share this research study with you because the participants were also connected to brain-imaging machines during the study and the researchers were able to detect differences in their brain activity while the participants were receiving the intervention. The group who received positive affirmations showed activation in the part of the brain that receives information and considers it self-relevant. For those who only received education, that part of the brain remained inactive. When I talk about this research in my training workshops, I try to put that in layman's terms. I typically say something like "Affirmations wake up the brain so that people will listen to the other cool stuff you say." Most of my audience members have the maturity to remember the old Charlie Brown cartoons. In them, the adults sound like "Woomp woomp woomp" rather than articulating words. Children can understand one another, but adults are essentially speaking a foreign and made-up language. I tell the folks I train, "When you try to teach people things they don't care about, you sound like the Charlie Brown mom. But when you affirm them first, you can more clearly communicate."

It matters *how* you compliment or affirm people. Listen to them and find the good in their words and actions. Otherwise, you're stuck with statements like "That's cool" and "Way to go!" You're missing an entire world of material out there by not really listening.

Rather than:	Try instead:
Good job!	*You didn't quit, even when it got hard.*
Way to go!	*You're so determined!*
That's awesome!	*It's awesome how you ask questions when you are confused.*
I'm proud of you!	*When I see how much you care about the world, I'm proud and inspired.*

Standard #2: Assert and Respect Boundaries

In my example of the board meeting, Santa Claus touched my body (boundary violation), commented on my appearance (boundary violation), and asked me for personal information (boundary violation). That sentence sure sounds strange if it is taken out of context!

Folks, there is a way to affirm the strengths you see in a person by only using the information they voluntarily share. But remember, boundaries go both ways. Sometimes, when people fish for compliments, they accidentally violate our boundaries (or attempt to). For example, I decided a long time ago that I was going to avoid complimenting weight loss that I noticed. That is a boundary I have set for myself because I don't want to place judgment on the shape of a person's body. But I can think of a time when I walked into a meeting and my colleague did a little dance, bragging, "Dr. Watson, look at me! I've lost twenty pounds!"

I held my breath for a second to keep myself from immediately falling into the trap. I would have been disappointed in myself if I had said, "You look fantastic!" So I paused and said, "You seem like you're really proud of your hard work."

She danced again and said, "You bet! This shit ain't easy!" Phew, I dodged that bullet. Don't allow other people to entice you into violating your own boundaries.

And by the way, there are so many ways to frame a compliment that don't include a comment on physical appearance:

- *You're so organized.*
- *You have the best book recommendations.*
- *I'm amazed by your leadership skills.*
- *You're innovative.*
- *You're a problem solver.*
- *You always motivate the team during morning practice.*
- *You give excellent gifts.*
- *You are a talented musician.*
- *You're always up for trying new things.*
- *You take such good care of the environment.*
- *You make the fluffiest pancakes.*
- *I don't know how you stay so calm under pressure, but it's impressive.*
- *You have a clever sense of humor.*
- *You give such clear directions. Thank you for that.*
- *You present yourself with such poise.*
- *You are a visionary.*
- *You're well-prepared for the camping trip.*

- *You are so in touch with your spiritual side. It's inspiring to me.*
- *You always remember to take care of your elders.*
- *I constantly learn from you.*
- *You listen so well. I always feel heard.*
- *You're a reliable person.*
- *You really stand up for yourself.*

Standard #3: Forgive Yourself for Not Reading Minds

When you compliment a person, you make an assumption about that person's values. If I say, "Wow, you are so tall! That's amazing!" I assume that height is something you value as a positive quality. If I say, "Gosh, you look so young for your age! What's your secret?" I assume that you value youth. In my story about the board meeting, Santa Claus complimented my appearance before I even said hello. He assumed that I would welcome his comment. Remember, Standard #3 is that you cannot read minds. We might try, but we are often pretty terrible at it, so tread carefully when you make assumptions about what to praise or affirm.

It's not the case that compliments based on appearance, age, or wealth are inherently ineffective, but there may be an implied message that is hurtful. What, for example, do we imply by telling someone, "Wow, you don't look your age! That's amazing"? While you may believe you are identifying attractiveness, you also imply that there is something wrong with aging. How many of us realize we communicate a message about our own values when we compliment a person for looking young?

Standard #4: Embrace Vulnerability

It may require vulnerability to find a person's strengths, even in their worst moments. When your guard is up and you're trying to protect against another person's ability to cause you discomfort, you may act aggressively out of desperation. My friend Carol's son struggled with a heroin addiction for years, and she worried about him so much that she'd constantly try to shake some sense into him. She'd say things like "You're going to end up dead!" and "You aren't living up to your potential!" and "You're going to hurt the entire family!"

These comments came from her desperate attempt to avoid her own grief that would come if he died. She was, of course, afraid, but acting in a way to protect herself from being both afraid *and* grief-stricken at the same time. To say to her son "My favorite thing about you is your sense of humor, and I miss that about you when you're high" would require her to lean into her love for her son, which feels risky. For Carol, it felt safer to get aggressive. She was putting on her armor.

Leaning into love is always difficult when you love someone who engages in risky behavior. No one wants to stick their heart out on the line for someone who might just break it. But seeing the good in people requires us to do that from time to time. It's radical vulnerability to say "I'm going to love all the best things about you, even though I feel you slipping away."

There will be times when you want to scream at a person, "Get your shit together!" because you cannot muster up the trust it requires to see the good in them. You have to trust that admiring their strengths will help them more than your desperate pleas for change.

I have a friend who copes with life while managing anxiety, ADHD, and a mountain of childhood trauma. I'm always trying to help him by introducing him to books, podcasts, and support groups. It's well-meaning. But maybe my behavior constantly reminds him he has problems to overcome. Maybe I could speak more to his strengths. Maybe I could call him up and say, "Man, you buy the best gifts for people. Where do you find those? I need a birthday gift for my friend, and I'm struggling. Can you help me?" Affirm his strengths and let him use his strengths. It's better than trying to fix what is wrong with him, and it's a far cry from a vague or superficial compliment like "You're cool. You're awesome. Way to go, dude."

This feels risky because I worry about him. My gut says that I should search for resources and interventions to solve his problems. Deep down, I want to be able to look in the mirror and say to myself, *You did everything you could*. That's what a person says when they're in warrior mode, with the armor on. It's more vulnerable to say, *He's dealing with a lot, but I'm going to trust that he will heal if I love him. I have no guarantee that things will get better with this approach, but I'm going to give it a chance anyway.*

Vulnerability would have allowed Santa Claus to sit and listen to me with respect. He would have been vulnerably realizing that a woman half his age was teaching him new things. He could have admitted that to me—even privately—and it would have felt like a genuine compliment. But in the absence of vulnerability, he attacked my credibility in a compliment disguised to make himself look like a jolly old man. *Smart cookie?* I couldn't have felt less like a smart person that day. The compliment made me feel like a fool. I never thought I would say this, but Santa can be a real pain in the ass.

Chapter 3:
Well-Meaning Apologies

"Never ruin an apology with an excuse."
—Benjamin Franklin

I have never met Stacey, but I feel like I know her. She's a friend of a friend, and she's basically all of us at once. Let's face it, she has permanently pulled her hair into a ponytail, she probably eats her lunches standing up, and I'll bet her e-mail inbox has reached its limit more than once.

After a long day of seeing patients at the hospital, Stacey pulled into her driveway on an icy January evening. She had been taking care of people all day, including the unit manager who can never seem to find the paperwork she needs. Stacey took a few deep breaths while sitting in her car, hoping to enjoy the air without the very clinical hospital smell. She thought to herself, *These might be my only peaceful moments today* while she trusted the front seat of her car to hug her tired bones.

When she finally dragged her feet up the sidewalk to the house and put her key in the lock, she heard her eight-year-old daughter announce to the entire house, "Mom's home!" Stacey had been discovered, so her plan to sneak in and hide was hopeless. She thought to herself, *I just need to sit down and eat. I've been on my feet all day.*

Stacey walked into her kitchen area where there was a pile of trash, a cup of spilled milk, and a trail of shoes and backpacks left from 3:30 when the kids got in. Annoyed, she released an exasperated call for her husband, "Andy?"

Andy strutted into the room, humming the theme song to *Paw Patrol*. Stacey rolled her eyes and thought, *Must be nice to have all that time to watch television with the kids.*

To the tune of the song, Andy playfully sang, "Paw Patrol! Paw Patrol! How was your day, babe?"

He was bouncy and cheerful—nothing like how Stacey felt after a long day of seeing patients. She answered in one short word: *Fine.*

Bowing down like a humble servant, Andy asked, "What do you want for dinner, my lady? I'll get it started." Stacey looked at her watch and exhaled dramatically.

"Sweetie, it's 8:30. You and the kids haven't eaten yet?"

Casually, he said, "Nah, they weren't hungry. Is everything okay, babe? Bad day?"

"Well, I thought you would have eaten, and I expected to just grab something to microwave. Instead, the kids haven't eaten, and they will want something before bed. Have they even done their homework? What have you been doing? Were you just watching TV? There is garbage everywhere and spilled milk. Andy, it's just so hard to come into this chaos. I know you had a busy day too, but you've been home since 3:30. I hate that I have to walk in at 8:30 and get everything in order. They need baths. I need to pack their school lunches. I'm exhausted."

Andy's eyes filled with tears. He said, "I'm so sorry."

He dragged on. "I never meant to let you down. I feel terrible. It's like I can't do anything right, and I'm not the man you deserve. You work so hard. You shouldn't have to come home to this, and I should know better. I feel like I'm turning into my dad, and that really scares me. I mean, it's *really* scary. I will make this up to you. I want everything to be okay, and I'm just so worried that I'm failing you."

Stacey let out a heavy sigh while aggressively running her hands through her hair, and then she fell into her normal pattern, consoling her guilt-ridden husband. "Baby, everything is fine. You're not failing me. And you're not your father. You're ten times the father he was. These kids adore you. These are just minor issues like dishes, laundry, and packing lunches. It's really not that big of a deal, and we'll tackle it together, okay?"

Stacey opened her arms, and Andy came in for a hug. She kissed his forehead and said, "I love you. Everything is going to be okay. Don't worry."

Andy, as it turned out, was just another person Stacey had to care for. He had good intentions, but his apology manipulated the situation, so he became the victim in need of care rather than the perpetrator who needs to reform. When you make a mistake, apologizing clearly and genuinely is one thing, but falling to pieces and asking your victim to put you back together is entirely inappropriate and cruel.

Through my training and consulting company, I offer coaching for social justice advocates who wish to use their positions of privilege for good rather than harm. When I coach individuals about using their privilege responsibly, we talk about how privilege creates power dynamics that result in mistrust, feelings of domination, and an overcommitment to being "good." Well-meaning white people, for example, who identify as "good white people" have a tough time when they realize their biases cause harm to people of color. When your identity is wrapped up in the belief that you are "good," it becomes very difficult to accept that you too have caused harm. In these moments, we see people fall to pieces. Fine. Shatter all you need to shatter, but don't ask the person you hurt to console you. That's cruel and unusual punishment to a person you've already injured. All you have to do is type "white tears" into a Google search box to read the hundreds, perhaps thousands, of articles that exist on this subject as it relates to racism. So instead, it's important to

1. reflect on your own harmful actions,
2. verbalize the words "I'm sorry" or "I was wrong,"
3. acknowledge the impact of your actions, and

4. take responsibility for changing your own behavior with no labor by the victim.

Rather than…	Try this instead…
"Oh my god! I feel terrible! I'm so mortified by my behavior! Will you please help me do better in the future? I feel like a monster!"	"I think I see where I went wrong. Thanks for helping me gain that insight. I'm dedicated to doing better in the future. I can figure this out on my own, but I welcome any suggestions you have."

And a strong apology—as genuine and considerate as it may be—is not a replacement for reparations or consequences. The apology is just a good start, but some harmful behavior also warrants resignation from a position of power or repayment for a damaged item or some kind of good deed or act of service. Andy should have said, "Stacey, put your feet up. I got this under control."

Despite a culture that seems at war with apologies, I would argue that we might all benefit from actively practicing the skill of apologizing with sincerity, clarity, and accountability. Let's run it through the four standards for guidance.

Standard #1: Listen More Than You Speak

When you are in a position where you need to apologize, remember this: It's not just that a wrong has been committed, but that a relationship has been strained. You will need to repair the relationship before anything else, and a good way to do that is to listen to the person you have harmed. Bear witness to their testimony. For centuries, we've known that for healing to happen, the truth must come out.

And it's difficult to listen well while you're feeling defensive of your own behavior. One requirement of listening well is suspending your urge to defend. For example, try not to say, "I'm sorry, but …" because once you introduce the word *but*, you reveal your defensiveness. Let your apology stand on its own even if you have other points to make rather than saying, "I'm sorry you're hurt, but you need to learn how to take feedback better." Both parts of that statement may be true, and you may, deep down, want to express both ideas. You do not, however, need to express them all in the same sentence. Why not let your apology get some attention before you emphasize a criticism of the other person? This may take more time, but how about this approach?

> "I'm sorry I shared your secret with Josh after you asked me not to do so. I hear you telling me that you feel betrayed. It's not okay for me to violate your trust, and I take that seriously. It's my responsibility to make this right. I'm going to work hard to deserve your trust in the future."

To apologize in this way requires that you listen to the person you have harmed.

Sorry is a word full of landmines attached to sour memories. But an apology is also how we repair relationships. And although US society prioritizes punishment and consequences *before* repairing relationships, I would argue that it should go the other way around. We know from the field of restorative justice that it is a mistake to impose a consequence and hope that the consequence somehow magically leads to a repaired relationship.

When teachers see two children fighting, they may assign them both detention and hope that they can get along in the future. But I see no pathway from violence to consequence to friendship. Instead, we need to help people prioritize their relationship first and foremost. When two children are fighting in the schoolyard, there is a harm to the community that needs repairing. The children may have harmed one another, and they may have disturbed their classmates. Each injured party needs to be heard. Each injured person deserves an apology and a chance to forgive. Of course, consequences may be part of the equation, but I suspect there would be no harm if we focused on relationships first and then determined the consequences if they are still necessary. This can be true in marriages, workplaces, and anywhere else where mistakes are made. Repair the relationship and then determine the consequences, if any.

Standard #2: Assert and Respect Boundaries

After you issue a sincere apology, it's important to detach yourself from whatever happens next because you have no control over how a person receives your apology. It's not up to you to decide whether your apology will lead to forgiveness. To respect boundaries is to respect that the injured party has every right to reject your apology and withhold forgiveness. The injured party owes you nothing.

Maybe you're the one waiting for an apology. If that's true, keep in mind that you could spend your entire life waiting for someone to apologize and take responsibility for the ways they've harmed you. If you hold on to that desire for closure and vindication, you will put the other person in charge of your growth, which is another way we violate our own boundaries.

Similarly, take responsibility for what exists within your own boundaries and accept the burden of repairing the harm. Don't say things like "Can you teach me how to do better in the future?" You know how to Google that shit. Do some work.

Standard #3: Forgive Yourself for Not Reading Minds

You can't genuinely show remorse for something if you don't know what you did. If someone is mad at you and you don't know why, ask for clarity before you apologize. Some people say, "I'm sorry for whatever I did." That's not sincere. It's perfectly acceptable to say, "It's clear that I've hurt you, so I owe you an apology. Because I want the apology to be as sincere as you deserve it to be, I need some clarity about the harm I've caused. Can you provide that for me? It will help me apologize in a more meaningful way, and you deserve that."

This is not the same as asking for education. In this case, you're not asking for a lesson for your own personal growth. Instead, you're asking to better understand the person you hurt.

Standard #4: Embrace Vulnerability

When a relationship has been strained, it's tempting for people to armor up to avoid getting hurt. I've received hundreds of examples from our podcast audience. Here are some:

- *I made a mistake at work, and rather than apologizing, I just started job searching. It felt easier to just sever ties.*
- *My boyfriend caught me in a lie, and he was willing to forgive me, but I couldn't handle the temporary tension between us, so I broke up with him.*
- *I had a fight with my best friend. Deep down, I knew I was wrong, but I just kept pointing out her flaws. In retrospect, I was really just mad at myself, and I took it out on her.*

When vulnerability isn't your thing, you go on the attack.

In US culture in particular, apologies feel risky because an admission of guilt can leave us vulnerable to heavy consequences in a litigious society. In fact, lawyers and insurance companies often caution against ever apologizing. A *New York Times* (2019) study found that US presidential candidates lose support when they offer public apologies. We are living in a society that actively opposes remorse, regret, and repair.

Accepting responsibility requires vulnerability because it's an acknowledgment that you are flawed. To do this well, avoid blaming the other person for your mistake. For example:

Rather than:	Try instead:
I'm sorry you misunderstood me.	I'm sorry we had a misunderstanding. Let me see if I can be clearer.
I'm sorry you took it the wrong way.	I'm sorry you are hurt. I did not expect that. I had a totally different intention, but unfortunately, you still ended up feeling hurt. I am really sorry about that.
I'm sorry you're mad.	I'm sorry my behavior made you mad.

Taking responsibility for your actions is a huge part of a sincere apology. But of course, there may be times when an apology is unnecessary. Sometimes people will make you believe you need to apologize for setting firm boundaries. Wrong. Take a look at these examples:

Apologize when:	No need to apologize for:
You have caused regrettable harm	Existing
You have violated a boundary	Having needs and wants
You were wrong about something	Having feelings
You acted outside of your own values or ethics	Having priorities and goals
You have broken trust	Needing help
You have let yourself down	Saying yes or no

What a complicated labyrinth we navigate when people are hurt. I hope you'll find that it's worth your time and your vulnerability to deliver the apology your friends and loved ones deserve.

Chapter 4:

Well-Meaning Advice

"This life is mine alone. So I have stopped asking people for directions to places they've never been."
—Glennon Doyle

Upon completion of my counseling graduate program, I hunted furiously for a job. With a determined heart, I submitted ten or twenty applications daily. I knew a few things for sure: I wanted to trade my life in New York for one in Philadelphia (where I grew up). I wanted to work somewhere for a year while I applied to doctoral programs. I knew it would be ideal if I could work at a university doing academic research, which was the experience I needed most.

I applied for hundreds of jobs with little response, leaving me feeling desperate and defeated. Finally, one day, I heard from a university where I was invited to interview for a job on a research study. Jackpot! This opportunity checked all my boxes!

From New York City, I took an early-morning train to Philadelphia for my interview. First, I was scheduled to meet with the person I would be replacing. She and I met for coffee, and it was immediately obvious that she was trying to warn me against taking the job. She wasn't overt about it, but I could read between the lines. She was trying to let me know the team is disorganized, stressful, and unproductive. But she hadn't totally scared me off because she was merely a stranger. For all I knew, she could have been a disgruntled employee. I wouldn't allow her to ruin my shot at joining this prominent university.

Next, I met with the principal investigator for the study. She was the decision maker, and she would be my boss if I took the job.

I waited for her in a dark and dusty hallway until I saw her rolling her wheeled briefcase down the hall, looking more like the nutty professor than I had expected. When she finally came to shake my hand, her first question was "Can you come back tomorrow?"

With a fake smile that would have made my mama proud, I politely reminded her that I took a train from New York for the interview and it would be impossible for me to repeat the trip the next day given other commitments I had to keep. After not getting her way, she let out a heavy sigh, and then she said, "Okay, well, wait here." I stood in the unair-conditioned hallway outside of her office for an hour. No one offered me water. No one offered me a chair. I did not know where to find the bathroom. I just stood there sweating in high heels, feeling nervous and annoyed.

Finally, her office door swung open. She popped her head out and laughed. "Oh my gosh, you're still here! Okay, go sit in there." She pointed inside her office. Stacks of paper covered every chair. I asked her if I could move something to create space. She said, "Yeah, sure." I gathered up stacks of paper and placed them on a table near the window.

She walked barefoot across the room to sit cross-legged in her own chair. She asked me, "Did I get a resume for you?"

I said, "I submitted one through the university's hiring process, but I'd be happy to offer you a fresh copy." I handed her a printout.

She said, "Oh. You went to Columbia? What do your parents do for a living?"

What? Are you kidding me? What do my parents do for a living? What does that matter?

I knew it was essentially a question about my social class, and I knew it was completely inappropriate, but I had to say something!

I had been tipped off by my coffee buddy from earlier that the PI "enjoys helping young people who are trying to get a start." I assumed that she wanted me to say something like "My parents were both dishwashers. I made it through Columbia on scholarships and grit." But that wasn't true.

My mom had been a schoolteacher but left for a career in finance a long time ago. My dad had been a bartender but left for a career in higher education a long time ago. I did not grow up poor and struggling, and this woman couldn't really save me the way she might want to. I was honest. I said, "My mom works in healthcare finance, and my dad is a professor at a local college."

Then she asked me about my marital status. Then she asked me how old I was. I wasn't dumb or naïve. I knew they were illegal questions to ask in an interview. I also knew that I wanted the job, so I played along.

A few weeks later, they invited me for a second interview. I took the train to Philadelphia again, and the moment I arrived at Thirtieth Street Station, the PI called me to reschedule. I turned around and went back to New York City. That happened to me at least one more time during this process.

After they had jerked me around for almost two months, I assumed they had moved on with another candidate, so I continued my job search elsewhere. Then I received a call from the PI. This time she was asking me for a writing sample, and she needed it in thirty minutes. I was sitting in the middle of Central Park. I got up, ran to my apartment at 114th and Amsterdam, and sent her the first academic paper I could find on my computer. I had no time to read it over and make edits. I just hit send and hoped for the best.

About thirty seconds after I hit send, my phone rang again. It was the PI one more time. In a rush, she spit out, "Don't worry about the writing sample. I don't need it. I'm going to send you an offer letter. The pay is not negotiable. We have a grant. Can you start on May 15th?"

This should have been a moment of glory. I should have been jumping up and down, celebrating that I was just offered this amazing research position after I had applied for hundreds of jobs in a depressed economy. But I felt uneasy. I took a deep breath and said, "Thank you so much. I look forward to reviewing the offer letter. Assuming that everything looks fine on the letter, I can begin work on May 19th. I graduate on May 18th, and I could leave New York that evening and begin work the next day."

She released another heavy sigh—like the childish one she had let out on the day of our interview. She said, "I really need you here on the 15th. I can give you the 18th off so you can go up to New York to graduate."

What was so important? I was already willing to grab my diploma and hit the road. Wasn't that enough?

I reiterated in my best kumbaya-ish soothing voice, "I'm so happy to hear from you, and I'd really like for us to move forward. Would it be okay if I took some time to review the offer letter and consider my graduation plans?"

She said, "Well, fine, but I really need to know."

I told her I understood the urgency and promised not to drag it out. We both hung up.

That evening, I spoke to a lot of friends and professional mentors. I don't know that I was seeking advice as much as I was seeking sympathy. I think I wanted everyone to say, "Oh, you poor thing. Isn't job searching miserable?" Instead, every single person said the same thing: *Do not take that job.* They knew, just like I did, that the PI seemed like a nightmare. Everyone kept saying, "Red flags, Kate. These are red flags." I knew that was true. But I also knew that I would not take their advice—I hadn't even been seeking it. I also knew this job had the potential to set me on a successful path in life. I was only planning to work there for one year anyway. This was just a stepping stone between graduate school and a doctoral program.

I took the job. It was just as awful as I thought it would be, and I have no regrets about putting myself through that. I defied everyone's advice, and thank goodness I did. Through that job, I met a faculty member at the nearby Drexel University who ultimately helped me apply for my doctoral program and later served on my dissertation committee. Because of that job, I traveled across the globe for training, where I met some of my best friends in the entire world. Because of that job, I facilitated my first real workshop, which has now become my full-time career and passion. Because of that job, I gained valuable research experience for my resume.

I feel proud that I defied everyone's advice. They didn't know what I needed or wanted. They only knew that the job sounded terrible. They weren't wrong about that, but they were missing the other pieces of the puzzle.

How I wished back then that just one person would say something like "Wow, Kate, that sounds like a tough situation. Obviously, only you can know what's best. What are you leaning toward right now?"

Why didn't my friends and mentors trust me to decide? They were trying to be helpful, but I could have used their votes of confidence more than I needed their advice.

Standard #1: Listen More Than You Speak

Sometimes helpers jump in with advice when all they really need to do is listen to what a person needs. If you can listen carefully enough to hear what a person says, means to say, and needs, you can help fulfill that need. Sometimes we assume we are being asked for advice when we are not. A person who says, "I don't know what to do" did *not* say, "Please tell me what to do." These statements differ in dramatic ways. Learn to hear them differently so you can ask, "Are you looking for advice, or do you want to sit with the uncertainty a bit?"

Keep in mind that just listening is really helpful. Sue Klebold is the mother of Dylan Klebold, one of the shooters at Columbine High School in 1999. Upon reflecting on her time parenting Dylan, she said, "I wish that I had had the ability to delve deeper and ask the kinds of questions that would've encouraged him to open up more to me. I had parented my kids, in many ways, the way I had been parented, which means you listen to your kids' problems and you try to fix them. I think what I needed to do with Dylan more was to just shut up and listen, to try to get him to say to me what he was feeling and thinking about something, rather than to automatically jump to a way to make him not feel that way or to fix the way he felt."

It takes practice to listen well enough to truly hear a person's intention rather than your own assumptions and biases. People are often saying so much more than their words. Consider these examples of statements and potential hidden meanings:

Person's words	Potential other meaning	Potential need
"I guess I don't know what to do next."	"I feel incompetent."	I need to feel confident.
"I know what you're saying, but…"	"You don't get it."	I need to be understood.
"Sure. Okay. Thanks. Whatever."	"I don't want to talk about it anymore."	I need to be alone now.
"I can't figure out which way I want to go with this."	"I have some options, and I'm deciding which one is best."	I need to keep giving this more thought.

I acknowledge that some people will directly ask for advice, but I would still act with caution because your advice could be terrible. When I made my first trip to the Middle East, I asked a friend who lived there, "Given the cultural expectation of modesty for women, what is appropriate for me to wear in public?" I directly asked for her advice. But she, believing she was helpful, kept saying, "Wear whatever you want. Who cares?"

After I checked with her a few more times, I ultimately decided that I must have been overthinking the whole thing, so I took her advice. I stepped out of her apartment in Dubai, wearing a sleeveless shirt and a skirt. I put a scarf in my purse as a precaution, and then we took a day trip to Abu Dhabi, where men on the street put their fingers in my face to express disapproval. Immediately, I felt regret and reached for my scarf to cover up. My friend pushed my hand out of the way and said, "Don't worry about them." But I *was* worried. More than anything, I worried about disrespecting the culture. When I look back on that experience now, I realize that she was giving the right advice for herself—I mean, she needed to live her life there. I can appreciate that, for her, it made little sense to make a home in a place where she was tiptoeing around. If she couldn't wear yoga pants and tank tops, she couldn't live there. But I was a visitor. I wanted to respect the culture. She was only trying to help me, but I ended up feeling uncomfortable and embarrassed because I took her advice.

Even though I asked for her advice, she probably could have acknowledged that her advice might not be appropriate for me, and she could have asked some clarifying questions to listen and understand my point of view.

Rather than . . .	She could have said . . .
"Wear whatever you want!"	"I can only tell you what works for me. What concerns do you have about using your normal wardrobe?"

Standard #2: Assert and Respect Boundaries

In the pilot episode of the TV series *This Is Us*, one of the main characters, Jack, sits teary-eyed on a bench in a busy hospital. He is eager to hear the status of his wife, who is delivering triplets. This particular scene takes place in 1980, so Jack is dressed a lot like my dad would have been back in his bartending days: shaggy hair, slim jeans, and mustache.

In the scene, an older man, Dr. Nathan Katowski, finds Jack in the hallway looking like a frantic parent who lost his child in an amusement park. He informs Jack that his wife is healthy and stable but that the third baby died during delivery. Jack jumps up from the bench and says, "I need to be with my wife."

Dr. Katowski replies in a calm and comforting voice, "And you will be. Soon. She needs some rest now." He gestures for Jack to have a seat on the bench. Then Dr. Katowski asks, "Is it okay if I keep you company a second?" Jack nods while he chokes down his tears. Then the doctor adds, "Is it okay if I attempt to say something meaningful?" With the slightest hope in his eyes, Jack nods in acceptance. With that permission from Jack, the doctor offers some perspective on life and death and how we hold people in our hearts long after they're gone. He speaks about how grief and loss in his own life have inspired him to save the lives of others. He took "the sourest lemon life has to offer and turned it into something resembling lemonade." By the end of his story, the doctor says, "I don't know if that was meaningful or senile, but I thought it ought to be said."

To me, the beauty of this scene is not the content of the message the doctor delivered. The beauty is in his asking permission to deliver the message at all. Asking permission does not need to be awkward or like a formal consenting process. Just like Dr. Katowski did in *This Is Us*, asking permission to share something can be both conversational and kind.

I can think of a time when a friend of mine called me to tell me about her terrible workday, and then she paused. I knew it was my turn to speak. I so badly wanted to say, "Wow, they do not appreciate you, and you should take your talents elsewhere. Get out of there. That place is making you miserable!" I didn't know, however, if she wanted any advice. Instead, I took a deep breath, and with as much transparency as I could offer, I described my thought process aloud: "You're obviously fed up with that place, and I don't blame you. I don't know, however, if you're interested in advice or if you just wanted me to know about the total fiasco."

She answered rapidly, "Oh, gosh, I'm already getting advice from all angles. I really don't need that right now. I just wanted to tell you because I know you've been aware of my ongoing struggles."

I validated her approach. I said, "Right, right. And if you hadn't filled me in, I might have mistakenly thought things were going well at work. Sometimes no news is good news, right? So I'm glad you are keeping me posted. What do you think you'll do next?"

Then she told me her plan. It was exactly the same plan I was going to advise her to make. She knew it on her own. She didn't need me to save her. She's a capable person. I'm glad I consulted with her before I launched into a useless speech.

Standard #3: Forgive Yourself for Not Reading Minds

Before you even consider doling out advice, I recommend you ask your friend (or spouse or colleague) what he or she already knows to avoid any risk of insulting the person's intelligence. When a friend told me, "I'm starting the keto diet next week," I wanted to warn her about all the potential side effects. Instead, I asked, "What have you learned about it?" She already knew everything I was going to tell her.

Much of what I know about giving advice I've learned from Miller and Rollnick's groundbreaking book, *Motivational Interviewing: Helping People Change*, where they make the case for respectful exchange of ideas between two people working together as partners. Borrowing from their work, I've developed this flowchart as an advice-giving model:

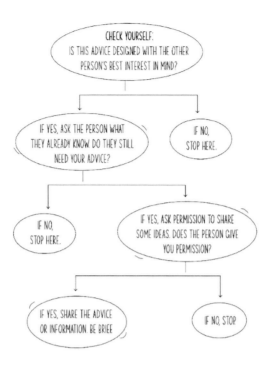

Standard #4: Embrace Vulnerability

Imagine leaving whatever building you're in right now to go outside. Imagine seeing a person outside smoking a cigarette. Imagine approaching that person and advising that person on strategies for quitting. I know what you're thinking: I would never do that! Of course, you wouldn't do that. Of course, you wouldn't assume that the person outside needs your advice or that the person is interested in your advice. In fact, you may even assume that the person is already knowledgeable about many ways to quit, and you might even trust the person to find strategies for quitting when they are ready to do so. That kind of trust is paradoxically easier with strangers. Somehow, it feels harder to trust our loved ones to learn and grow without our advice. It feels vulnerable to trust people. Giving advice says, "I didn't think you could figure this out," while patience shows "I'm pretty sure you got this."

Rather than . . .	Try this instead:
"I think you should _____."	Say in your own head, "This person is capable. I trust this person to figure it out."
"Why don't you just _____?"	"I want so badly to be helpful, but I'm sure you already know, deep down, what to do. I completely trust you to figure it out. You've done it before."

I'm a member of several professional organizations, which hold annual conferences. One year, I traveled to a conference in Atlanta, where I met someone from my hometown of Philadelphia. She suggested that upon returning home, we should meet up for coffee. I agreed. It certainly made sense to me that I should embrace colleagues who live right in my neighborhood as much as I embrace those who are spread around the planet. A few weeks later, we kept our agreement and had coffee in Philadelphia. I learned that she is a clinician and her specialty is substance abuse. While we were sitting in that café, she made several offensive and inappropriate remarks. She said things like "I don't work with women because, you know, they're all drama. So I only see men in my work." She added, "All addicts are trying to get one over on you" and "I can't stand dealing with students. They suck up all my time with their neediness."

I mostly enjoyed my coffee, nodded, and wondered, *How long do I have to sit here before I can leave?* Eventually, I used another meeting as my excuse to bow out of this coffee date. When she saw me reaching for my coat and my bag, she quickly blurted out, "The real reason I wanted to meet with you is because I think I could be an excellent mentor for you, Kate. I'd be happy to do it! I'm here for you anytime you need anything!"

Mentor for me? Folks, before you offer guidance and advice to people, make sure you're in a suitable position to offer it. She was not.

When I was a counselor, people would ask me, "How do you know what advice to give people?" My answer? "I never give advice." In my coaching work, clients thank me for "all the great advice," and then I reveal to them, "I gave you none." Sometimes my friends will ask me for advice, and I have to remind them that I ate cookie dough for breakfast and I've been wearing the same sweatpants for three days. Am I really in a position to advise others? I think not.

Chapter 5:

Well-Meaning Tough Love

We have enough people who tell it like it is—now we could use a few who tell it like it can be.
—Robert Orben, American comedy writer

As a public speaker, I'm afforded the opportunity to travel the world, sharing my research and skills with all kinds of humans doing wonderful work. I've been lucky to speak to audiences in South Korea, Poland, Germany, Belgium, Ireland, Japan, and more recently, Cuba. I traveled to Havana to speak at a medical anthropology conference right before the COVID-19 pandemic abruptly halted all my journeys. They were interested in hearing about my research with sexual assault responders in communities across the United States.

During my journey, I toured a coffee plantation in Las Terrazas, a self-sustaining eco-community in Cuba. In the Sierra del Rosario mountain range, Las Terrazas spans the provinces of Artemisa and Pinar del Rio.

My tour guides were Mariana, a young Cubana who spoke three or four languages better than I can speak English, and Eric, who could name every bird passing by in the jungle. He even matched their bird sounds so perfectly that I was convinced they were engaged in a full intellectual conversation. He was like a Cuban Tarzan or Dr. Dolittle.

Mariana and Eric brought me to the rural village of Rancho Curujey, where I learned about the village's reforestation efforts, and as a highlight of the day, we ate a delightful meal at La Casa del Campesino, an open-air restaurant positioned right in the middle of the jungle. It was not a bad way to spend my last few days of freedom before a year-long global lockdown.

All the bird sounds and eco-friendly stuff were cool and all, but let's get real: I showed up for the coffee. I'm normally a hot coffee kind of gal—the darker and stronger, the better—but the weather was warm, and Eric insisted I sit with him in the local café to enjoy a refreshing *café helado* (known to English speakers as iced coffee). I obliged, and I'm thrilled I did. Not only was the iced coffee delicious and decadent, filled with chocolate and thick cream, but also, while we were indulging in coffee heaven, Eric said something I would never forget.

He explained the evolution of the coffee plantation and described the clay tiles the builders used to construct the roof of the adjacent farmhouse. He mentioned, just in passing, that the builders intentionally left the clay a bit wet and soft in the middle before completing the process because the tile is stronger when it's soft on the inside.

Several minutes had passed, and we had completely changed subjects, but I asked, "Could you say that to me again? The part about the clay tiles?"

Eric looked really surprised, as if maybe no one had ever really listened to his story about clay before. I smiled, as if to say, *Yes, Eric, it's the moment you've been waiting for your entire life. Someone cares about your clay tile story enough to hear it twice.*

He spoke with the excitement of a child at his sixth birthday party. He explained, "If you put clay in the oven with the persistent fire inside, the tile will break. The tile can withstand stronger storms if it's not too stiff in the middle." I sat back in my chair, put my hand on my chin in a thinking gesture, and added, "It's like how trees blow in the wind." Then Eric smiled, even bigger than when he was chatting with the birds, because we too were speaking the same language. He slowly nodded in agreement and said, "That's right. When trees don't bend a bit, they're more at risk of falling over. They are stronger when they're flexible."

Folks, soft is not weak. Even Mother Nature agrees.

Very often we mistakenly believe that a show of force will help awaken people to changes we believe they need to make, and we call it tough love. We mistakenly believe we can help people by pushing and shoving them toward change. Our guts tell us to be forceful, but we, just like clay tiles, are stronger and more effective when we are gentle and flexible.

The Cubans are not the only ones who know this. I learned from my Irish ancestors that we ought to be strong in the mind and soft in the heart. So let's rethink "tough love," shall we?

Standard #1: Listen More Than You Speak

Sometimes people brag about being "brutally honest" or "keeping it real" when, in reality, they were just using their truth bombs to be malicious and arrogant. Those same people like to complain that their friends and family members "can't handle the truth," but I can't even handle cupcakes and doughnuts if they're being shoved down my throat against my will. The implication here is that the helper believes she understands something that the helpee does not, and the helper is ready to force-feed this information to the helpee, who is an unwilling or uninterested participant in the conversation. Sometimes a person's brutal honesty is really a sign that they have lost their cool and they are not listening.

I'm talking about those times when Person A believes something and Person B disagrees. Person B might be tempted to "truth bomb" Person A with "brutal honesty" and call it "tough love." Let's use the example of my friends Kelly and Brendan, who were recently talking about climate change.

Brendan's Position	Kelly's "Tough Love" Response
I'm not sure that climate change is real. I feel like we need more research to better understand it. There's just not enough out there yet.	I'm just going to shoot straight with you: That's insane. I'm sorry, but there is no way to sugarcoat it for you. Climate change is a conclusion based on observations of a great many global indicators. The clearest evidence is the surface temperature record. Even though most analyses only go back 150 years, we have some records going back several centuries.

Kelly may feel a moment of intellectual superiority and moral purity, but with this approach, she isn't helping Brendan understand climate change any better. Kelly is like a lot of us who feel a huge responsibility to represent an entire group of people (in this case, environmentalists) when we come face-to-face with someone who challenges our beliefs. We feel concerned that our own insecurities will be exposed and we may disappoint other members of our tribe (again, in this case, the tribe might be environmentalists). A lot of "truth bombs" are intended to impress the people who already agree with us, not to change the mind of the person who disagrees. In other words, Kelly's rant was more about representing her tribe than it was about helping Brendan better understand climate change. She got to feel like a good environmentalist, which may be rooted in her need for belonging. Meanwhile, Brendan is no closer to understanding her point of view.

Kelly could have helped Brendan by listening first and allowing him some dignity and psychological support. But to do this feels threatening to Kelly because she wants to belong to her tribe. But understanding a person, no matter how wrong they are, cannot hurt you.

To illustrate this concept, I like to think about oncologists. I have no doubt that oncologists hate cancer—probably more than anything in the world. Of course, they do. Yet they spend their entire lives trying to better understand cancer. None of them worry that the act of understanding cancer will be misconstrued as an endorsement for cancer, for they know understanding cancer is the only way to fight it. The same is true for people who disagree with you politically, religiously, or morally. If you want any hope of changing a person's point of view, you will have to understand it first. And understanding is not the same as endorsing. It's okay to lean in a little, even though your nature is to defend. I'm not asking you to coddle people. Instead, I'm asking you to deliver your honesty and truth with the dignity that all humans deserve. To find that kind of compassion, you need to listen. If your tribe doesn't understand that, that's their problem.

Standard #2: Assert and Respect Boundaries

Remember, boundaries separate what belongs to me from what belongs to you. Imagine boundaries surround you like a physical fence or a wall. The ideal boundary is a sturdy fence with a gate.

The owner of the boundary decides when to open the gate and when to close it. Ideally, the owner of the boundary would only open the gate out of a genuine desire to help another person, not out of fear of consequence or punishment. For example, I draw a boundary for phone calls late at night. For the most part, I will not answer a phone call past 9:00 p.m. I might, however, make an exception if my parents were to call beyond the 9:00 p.m. cutoff. I do that because I love them, not because I'm scared they will be mad at me. You might say that when it comes to phone calls, I close the gate at 9:00 p.m., but the door can always be opened when necessary. It's a healthy boundary because I'm in control of managing it.

Some people have a very permeable boundary. It's too flexible. It's like a wiry or broken fence. Everything gets in. They don't assert or protect their boundaries. For example, my friend recently made an offer to her sister. She said, "I could come over and watch the kids while you run to the grocery store, if you'd like." My friend's sister gladly accepted the offer, but she added, "I will probably use that time to go to the grocery store, get my haircut, and visit with a few friends. Thanks for watching the kids!" My friend was stuck at her sister's house for an entire day because she didn't assert a boundary. My friend's fence doesn't seem to have a gate to close. People can just barge right in.

Others have a brick wall with no way in. These people are closed off and rigid. They have strict rules, and they often avoid intimate relationships with others. This can be a lonely life.

Rigid boundaries come to mind when people talk about tough love. It makes me think of the concept of "canceling" people, which is a pattern I'm worried about.

The pattern is as follows:

1. Observe a person do something terrible.
2. Publicly shame the person and rally a group to "cancel" the wrongdoer.
3. Many people hurl insults at the wrongdoer. They disconnect from the wrongdoer on social media.
4. Congratulate oneself for adequately punishing the wrongdoer.
5. The wrongdoer endures harsh consequences: isolation from society, career damage, etc.
6. The wrongdoer brews resentment and anger in isolation, but the world remains otherwise unchanged.

The cancel culture has well-meaning roots, but I'm not convinced that it leads to a better or safer world. It started as a push for more accountability in society, which is a noble cause. Unfortunately, some have co-opted and perverted the phrase to turn themselves into victims and dodge accountability. In a patronizing tone, they say, "Oh boy, here comes cancel culture!"

Others have co-opted and perverted the phrase as a rallying cry to destroy anyone who fails to align with current popular perspective. Can we all agree that we want to live in a society where people are held accountable for their actions? I hope so.

In reality, people behave better toward others, toward the earth, and toward themselves when they have both internal and external resources that are positive and uplifting. Tony Ward's Good Lives Model (www.GoodLivesModel.com) asserts that while wrongdoers have "obligations to respect other peoples' entitlements to well-being and freedom, they are also entitled to the same considerations" regarding human rights and dignity. The Good Lives Model, supported by decades of research, promotes individual and collective capacity building as a way of reducing a person's risk of re-offending behavior.

In other words, when a person has committed a wrong, we can reduce the likelihood of repeated offenses by connecting the offender to resources for self-improvement and growth, not harsh punishment or shame. We need to be careful not to cause more harm with the so-called tough love.

People who are punished with isolation become more likely to cause harm to society. Let's hold people accountable without imposing isolation (cutting them off, disconnecting on social media, etc.).

People who are punished with job loss become more likely to cause harm to society. Let's hold people accountable without destroying their economic security. The world is no better off when people suffer economically.

People who are punished with shame and public humiliation become more likely to cause harm to society. Let's hold people accountable without public humiliation and shame.

Mature societies can hold people accountable for their actions without removing all their resources and strengths. And they will do so—not because we wish to coddle harmful people—but because it ultimately creates a safer world for the vulnerable people who fear repeated victimization by wrongdoers.

Years back, my friend Dan would speak about people receiving public assistance using stigmatizing and undignified terms. He would say things like "It must be a welfare check time. There was a line outside the nail salon." One day, in response to one of his usual remarks, I said, "It seems like you are really interested in how people use their public assistance. Do you know anyone who qualifies for public assistance?" He looked up from the game he was playing on his phone. He looked at me and waited silently, like he expected me to apologize for my comment. I waited too. I can play this game. Eventually, he said, "I'm not trying to be a dick or anything."

I said, "You're worried that your comments are insensitive."

He fired back an inaccurate statistic: "Half of the people on food stamps abuse it! They sell them for money to buy alcohol. Bet you didn't know that!"

Knowing that the payment accuracy of SNAP benefits is 96 percent (and the food stamp trafficking rate is only 1 to 1.5 percent), I asked him to cite his source. I said, "I'm wondering where you read that."

He said, "You know what? Forget it, okay?"

Dan didn't speak to me for some time. I thought maybe he had "canceled" me because I asked him to explain his comments, and perhaps he didn't like to be challenged. Down the road, at a mutual friend's birthday party, I approached him. I said, "Hey, I haven't seen you in a while. Are we okay?"

He said, "You tell me. You got all snappy with me that time I told a joke."

"Dan, you made a claim, and I asked you to explain your claim. We could have had a discussion about it. You didn't want to. As far as I'm concerned, we're okay. I like hanging out with you, and sometimes I think you're a funny guy. But if you're telling jokes and I don't understand them, I'm going to ask you to explain. That has to be okay."

He seemed relieved that I hadn't cast him off to the land of offensive dudes. I was willing to spend time with him, but I promised to keep holding him accountable for his claims. He agreed to those terms. From that point forward, I would press him to explain himself, but I never canceled him. I really believe we both won in this scenario. Dan got to redeem himself by being more thoughtful about his biases, and I got to keep my friend. Some might say that Dan's comments make him irredeemable. Well, I hope that's not true because everyone I know has biases. I would argue that Dan is the best kind of friend to have because he is becoming aware of his biases in a way that a lot of self-proclaimed "woke" people are not.

When I hear people say "Person A offended me, so let's ruin him" or "Person B did something I don't like. Destroy her," I get worried. We may make a dangerous person more dangerous by taking away their capacities for a good life. The least dangerous person is one who has a good life to protect. I made sure Dan left that birthday party with a friendship intact. Isolating and humiliating him would not have been helpful for him, for me, or for society at large. We've all done unforgiveable things, and we all deserve some love (and not the tough kind).

However, I wouldn't necessarily recommend offering more love and kindness than you're able to give. You will, over the course of your life, meet people who cause you deep harm, and even though *someone* should care for that person enough to help them change, *you* do not need to be that person. Again, this is where boundaries come into play.

Ask yourself, "Am I the right person to help this person change? Or am I too hurt?" If you're too hurt, you might not be able to show the patience and support he/she will need to change. If you're able to, however, seize that opportunity. Sometimes I think to myself, "You know what, I'm actually in a good position to help this person change his ways because I'm bothered, but I'm not personally injured. I'm exactly the right candidate to help this person improve rather than just canceling him." That's how we use privilege for good, not harm. It's a privilege to be bothered, but not personally injured. I was bothered by Dan's joke, but not personally injured. I was the perfect person to challenge him. As far as I'm concerned, the people who would have been personally injured by Dan's joke are off the hook. I'm honored to advocate on their behalf.

In one of my social circles, for example, we have a member who tends to be dramatic and draining, and he demands so much attention from everyone. If he's there, you can bet that there will be a moment in the get-together when everything focuses on him and his troubles.

Sometimes the group doesn't even want to invite him because he derails the fun. But I take a moment to pause and ask myself, "Do I want him to change his ways? Or do I just want him to go away?" I want him to get better. So I ask myself, "Am I in a position to do this? Or am I too hurt?" The answer is "I can do it."

He's a friend, and I'm capable of showing him the love he needs to live a positive life. I don't need to cancel him. I think I can help him feel more secure and potentially even find some happiness. Since I may be one of the few people who can muster up some patience for him, I feel like I ought to capitalize on that. Maybe, compared with his other friends, I'm in a better position to support him. But that doesn't make me better than them. Maybe it just means I'm the one who has been hurt by him the least. It wasn't my birthday party he ruined. It wasn't my secret he shared. It wasn't my promise he broke. I'm bothered by his behavior, but I'm not personally injured. For that reason, I'm well-positioned to be good to him.

I used to have another friend who matched a similar description. Let's call him Kevin. He has many of the same qualities as the first friend I described, but I can't help him because he has hurt me too much over the years. I'm more than bothered by Kevin. I'm injured. He deserves a friend, but because I can't be that friend, I have mostly cut ties with him. I set a boundary. I guess some might say that I canceled him, but I disagree. Kevin is not canceled—my friendship with him is. Kevin has other friends. They can step up and support him now that I'm stepping back. He is in good hands—just not my hands. Jim Carey once said, "Just because you lost me as a friend doesn't mean you gained me as an enemy. I'm bigger than that. I still wanna see you eat, just not at my table." That, to me, is how we set healthy boundaries without canceling people.

Standard #3: Forgive Yourself for Not Reading Minds

When I hear people say, "He just needs some tough love," I am reminded that we don't know what other people need. You may never know if someone in your life is crying out for a hug, for some space, or for a kick in the ass. I'm not asking you to know something you cannot know. I'm only asking you to play the odds. Odds are the person needs a partner and a support, not a drill sergeant. If I'm wrong, you can always decide later to be the drill sergeant. I would, however, make the confrontational and aggressive approach your last resort because it's really difficult to reverse the order. Once you have confronted, attacked, or humiliated someone, it's almost impossible to reverse course and try to lead with love and empathy instead. It may be, at that point, too late. The damage is done. So play the odds.

Standard #4: Embrace Vulnerability

It requires vulnerability to accept people warmly, especially if they oppose your morals or values. This may be part of the reason we are so divided in this world. When we meet someone who holds a divergent viewpoint, our own intellectual safety feels threatened. We panic and go into fight-or-flight survival mode. We much prefer to surround ourselves with people who feel like protectors. Psychologist George Kohlrieser calls those protectors a "secure base" for connection (Kohlrieser, "Unleash Potential as a Secure Base Leader"). Without that secure base, we feel like our own values are under attack, but it's a delusion. Being near someone who disagrees with me poses no real threat to my well-being.

I learned this in graduate school when we had a lot of practice speaking to groups of people who disagree and who might even say some cringe-worthy things. We had to learn to tolerate them. But first, a little background—before graduate school, I was someone who valued equity and justice (just as I do today), but I was overly focused on harmony, color blindness, and treating everyone the same. Even as the cultural events planning chair of our university student government board, I was incredibly misguided. I relied on materialistic and purely symbolic gestures of unity and inclusion. I spent student money to organize salsa dance lessons and an Irish festival full of shamrocks and pots of gold. I'm embarrassed by the way I reduced cultural experiences down to what can be easily consumed by the dominant society, and I missed such an obvious opportunity to educate the student body about inequities and injustices.

Then I went to graduate school, where I had my ass kicked (in a supportive environment). We were required to take a course called Racial Identity Laboratory. It was five hours per week, for fifteen weeks, of intensive exploration of our racial identities. A lot of shit was said in that room. Real shit. Ugly shit. Hateful shit. Some of it was said in a nice, singsongy voice so it didn't sound so bad, but at the end of the day, we were, on a weekly basis, walking into that classroom to unload all the bullshit the world had taught us about power structures in society. Things are really fucked when it takes fifteen weeks just to sort out a small fraction of the ways you've been damaged by the world.

The most profound day of class occurred when our professor, a renowned psychologist who identifies as a white woman, looked at each of us in the room—mostly white women with a lot of privilege at an Ivy League school—and told us, "I really believe that racism is in the air that we breathe. I inhale racism, and I exhale racism. Our world is designed to make sure I keep repeating that cycle and that you do too. We are not supposed to even notice, but I am deeply and profoundly hurt by the racism that lives in me. It's an injury to my humanity. And the only path to healing exists where patient people are willing to love me through it. They didn't shame me. They saw the damage in me, and they loved me until I worked through it. It's the only way it's ever been done."

Folks, you can take her words, remove racism, and replace it with a lot of things that would still make sense. Replace it with fear. Replace it with anxiety. Replace it with any form of violence: sexism, classism, or homophobia. It remains true that we can be injured by these things and need healing more than we need tough love.

Now think of that person in your life whom you would love to "call out" and whose behavior is highly problematic. Rather than seeing an asshole, see the injured person. Rather than seeing someone who is rude, see someone who has been harmed. Rather than seeing someone who is obnoxious, see someone who has been damaged. We are all that injured person, and our injuries show when we are awful to others. When I see a person gossiping and putting people down, I see a person who has probably been bullied. When I see a person who flaunts their wealth or possessions, I see a person who has probably been made to feel worthless on the inside. We are all hurt people going around this big world, hurting other people, and we are unlikely to become any kinder after being called out, ostracized, and humiliated with tough love. Instead, we are likely to become more injured and later cause more harm. We need more love, not the tough kind.

I believe my professor was cautioning us against the "call out" culture (another term for a type of tough love) because it promotes the practice of publicly shaming people who have committed a wrong. I worry that "calling people out" only makes otherwise well-meaning people afraid to speak up. The wounds of racism, sexism, and classism will not heal in hiding. Shane Claiborne said, "Peace making doesn't mean passivity. It is the act of interrupting injustice without mirroring injustice, the act of disarming evil without destroying the evildoer, the act of finding a third way that is neither fight nor flight but the careful, arduous pursuit of reconciliation and justice. It is about a revolution of love that is big enough to set both the oppressed and the oppressors free" (Claiborne, Wilson-Hartgrove, and Okoro 2010).

Some experts recommend that we "call in" instead. They recommend that we privately initiate a conversation with someone whose behavior is problematic or hurtful. By calling in, we attempt to build a compassionate relationship with this person—one in which to grow and learn rather than publicly shame.

I know this approach disproportionately benefits people of privilege because it affords them comfort and kindness to patiently explore their biases, mistakes, and behaviors while the rest of us are out here trying to survive through discrimination, violence, and fear. That's why I don't expect everyone to participate in the "calling in" approach. I consider "calling in" the Cadillac treatment for racism, sexism, and classism, and it requires so much vulnerability to achieve it. It's the most effective, but not everyone can give that kind of treatment, and not everyone can receive that kind of treatment. There are times when I will say, "I know I should probably 'call this person in,' but I don't have it in me." I know my limits.

Ideally, calling in would be implemented by allies and advocates who haven't been so traumatized and harmed by the injustice they wish to end. They would be good candidates for a compassionate approach because they are less likely to be personally wounded by the injustice. Again, this is how we can use privilege for good, not harm. Practice "calling in" when you're bothered, but not injured.

In all areas of life, we mistakenly believe that we might "shake" a person into being better or doing better if we shame them first. It might sound like these:

"You wouldn't want to put your family through that, would you?"

"Can't you see how you've impacted your kids? They're watching you and learning from you. Is that what you want?"

"What kind of mother brings her noisy children to this restaurant?"

"Why would you go shopping on Thanksgiving night? Don't you care about the people who have to work at the store?"

These statements are shaming, and they are intended to make a person feel small. Shame correlates with many things we hope to help people avoid: overeating, under-eating, substance abuse, attempted suicide, and violence (as victim or as perpetrator) (Brown, 2013). That means that when we think we're "only trying to help," we may be actually making things worse.

Folks, you may look around your world at your friends, family members, and colleagues, and you may at times feel like you want to shake them and scream at them because of their poor choices or risky behavior. Remember, we can disagree about many things, but only compassion and love will help people change. The same is true for people who have done terrible things. It's not easy, but it is best to "hate the sin and love the sinner." Although "tough love" may feel like the best option, a softer and kinder love will often get you further. A recent subject of the popular Humans of New York blog said, "Everyone is either showing love or crying out for it." Remember that when you are trying to help your own friend. That person is in their own way crying out for love. How do you want to provide it? The tough way? Or a little soft inside?

Chapter 6:

Well-Meaning Humor

The bad thing about being a famous comedian is that, now and then, someone approaches me to tell an old joke. Don't tell me jokes—I have that. People also say the weirdest things, sometimes sarcastic things, and even evil things. They like to provoke to get a reaction.
—Robin Williams

I'll never forget the time I was warming my coffee in the employee lounge of the university where I conducted research and my colleague entered the room, looking a bit frazzled. As I waited for the last few seconds to tick off the microwave timer, I said, "Hey, there you are! Tell me about your date last night."

She shook her head and exhaled deeply. "Kate, I farted when I was in bed with him."

With hot coffee in my mouth, I still pulled off a sympathetic gasp. "Oh my god. What did you do next?"

She said, "We both started laughing hysterically. We weren't in a romantic mood anymore, but we talked all night. We traded embarrassing stories and laughed so much that my side hurts this morning. I may have strained my jaw! I really like him, and I can't wait to see him again."

I love that story so much. I think about it all the time. I lost touch with her, but damn, I hope she married that man, and I hope they laugh together long into their golden years.

The movie *Patch Adams* postures that laughter is the best medicine. I can certainly think of times in my life when a good belly laugh saved me from despair. Like the time I was having an argument with a partner and he very immaturely stomped his foot on the floor like a child. It was so utterly ridiculous that I stopped feeling angry, I laughed until I cried, and then I made fun of his poor coping skills relentlessly. He laughed too, and we were both in a much better position to solve our argument peacefully and productively because we *liked* each other again. For the next few weeks, I'd tease him with "Hey, I've got some bad news. Don't go stomping your feet on me!" And fortunately for me, he was a great sport about it.

Scientists have studied the healing properties of humor for decades. Because of their research, we know that humor has similar effects on the brain as drug-induced euphoria and that a moment of levity can also stimulate the release of dopamine, the feel-good neurotransmitter (Force, 2018). The Association for Applied and Therapeutic Humor is an organization focused on "the study and application of humor to effect positive change" (www.aath.org). Its website offers valuable information about the benefits of humor. "The strategic use of humor sparks connection, increases influence, improves communication and can be used as a competitive advantage in any industry. What's more, humor provides innumerable benefits to our overall health and well-being, including reduced stress, greater resilience, decreased depressive symptoms, and even increased pain tolerance."

So sure, laughter is healing, but it is not a panacea. Realistically, there is no such thing as a treatment that cures everything. Even the most effective pills have limitations and side effects. I think that's true of humor as well.

People talk about how comedians get famous laughing about their own tragedies. Comedy can, as we know, serve as a kind of drug for people in turmoil, and much like other painkillers, people can get addicted to the painkilling effects of comedy. They can even develop a tolerance, whereby they need bigger and more outrageous and shocking humor to get the same impact. If you rely on humor to be your medicine through tough times, fine, but there will come a time when the jokes just can't give you the high you need to feel better, and a lot of funny people hit that wall at some point.

So I worry about people who rely exclusively on their sense of humor to get through tough times. One of the earliest psychological studies of comedians, completed in 1975 by Samuel Janus of New York Medical College, surveyed fifty-five successful full-time comedians. Janus found that 80 percent of the comedians had sought psychotherapy for psychological distress. Interestingly, he commented in his article that comedians "repeatedly expressed the fear that if they were successful in [treatment], to the point where their suffering was greatly relieved, they would then cease to be funny."

So this begs the question, what is the relationship between comedy and well-being? Is it that comedy leads to positive well-being as *Patch Adams* taught us? Or that poor mental health leads to comedy as Janus's research participants seemed to hint? I won't pretend to know the answer to that question since it is unlikely a causal relationship, but I will further complicate the question by citing the *International Journal of Cardiology*'s conclusion that comedians have an overall lower life expectancy than people who are not comedians, which raises a new question: Is it possible that comedy somehow negatively affects health?

Let's put it this way: Even if laughter is the marvelous medicine so many of us believe it to be, maybe it can only heal so much before it harms. The Italians have a saying, *Una risata vi seppellirà*, which translates to "It will be a laugh that buries you." And let's not forget that the Weasels (from the movie *Who Framed Roger Rabbit?*) literally died laughing. This is serious.

So I try to look out for the times when comedy, as delightful as it may be, can get us into trouble. I avoid using comedy like a drug to cover up discomfort, and I remain mindful of the times when the people I love may be misusing humor to mask pain. Being helpful means allowing people to remove the comedic mask.

A couple of years ago, following several difficult workweeks, I was out in Center City Philadelphia, cashing in on a deal I had made with myself: survive these stressful weeks, hit all my goals, finish all my projects, and as a reward, I could go on a mini shopping spree. The hurdles before me included delivering lectures in two countries and five states, finishing a draft of my dissertation proposal to share with my committee, grading final exams for an undergraduate research methods course, and completing a full marathon without dying. From the lectures to the long-distance run, I left every checkpoint in my dust, so I felt deserving of that stroll down the Walnut Street retail corridor. As I recall, I almost dared to walk into Tiffany & Co., so I must have been feeling like Julia Roberts from *Pretty Woman*. I got a manicure. I bought new shoes. I slowly sipped a glass of wine over lunch. And just as I was performing a sniff test on some candles at Bath and Body Works, my phone vibrated. I glanced down. It was a text from my friend Ravi.

"I hate everything about my life."

Shit. I knew Ravi was prone to mood swings, so this kind of abrupt message wasn't completely out of character for him. Because I had been practicing my boundary-setting, I decided to wait to respond when I could be in a better headspace and a quieter environment. So I passed on the candles, left the store, and walked a few blocks to a local park where I knew it would be less crowded and chaotic. As soon as I sat down on the bench, my phone vibrated again. It was another text from Ravi.

"I'm in a dead-end career. I think my wife hates me, and she's probably going to leave me. I'm a terrible father. I really shouldn't have had kids at all. I'm overweight, and I'm in debt, and I've lost touch with most of my friends."

I still had not replied. I knew I was going to need some serious coping skills to get through this conversation, so I drank a few sips of my water, took several deep breaths, and very intentionally relaxed my shoulders, jaw, and eyebrows. As I usually do when I'm about to do something that feels vulnerable and tense, I delivered myself a little pep talk.

In my head, I thought, *He's a good friend, and he needs you, Kate. Time to show up. He's in pain, but don't look away. Ravi, like all people, deserves a space to be real.*

Okay, I was ready to support him, even though it meant taking my heart on a trip to Sadtown. I offered via text, "Hey, friend. You have so much on your plate right now. And you're at a point where you need something to change. You're ready for that. Would you like to meet up so we can talk more?"

With little time for pause, Ravi replied, "Nah, I'll just crap my pants, wear hippie pajamas all day, and get it the hell over with."

Was that a joke? I really couldn't tell whether he was trying to make me laugh or he was really that depressed. When I can't easily read the room, I usually tread lightly.

"It's really not an inconvenience to meet up. I'm just out shopping. No big deal."

He followed up with "Shopping? Oh, good, pick out some good pajamas for me for when I go to the nuthouse, will ya? Throw in some fuzzy socks." He attached a picture of Jack Nicholson's character from *One Flew Over the Cuckoo's Nest.*

At that point, I knew he was making jokes, but they weren't funny. I had given myself the pep talk to not look away from his pain, and I was trying to deliver on that promise I made to myself. I was bravely standing there, ready to feel some serious stuff with him, and obviously, we were in different places emotionally. I was being vulnerable. He was the one looking away. He was the one too afraid to feel difficult feelings. I went from having a glorious day to feeling concern for my friend, and now he wants me to be goofy? It's like emotional whiplash. He invited me into Sadtown and then left me there while he ran off to fake Happyville.

Once I gained a little perspective, I realized that Ravi needed to find his own readiness to face difficult things. Just because I was feeling ready and brave doesn't mean that he was, and it's my job to have boundaries around that. Maybe I shouldn't have gone so far into Sadtown without an escape plan. I got left behind, and that's not entirely Ravi's fault.

So if Ravi needs to crack jokes to mask his discomfort, fine. I can't make him brave enough to be vulnerable. I can't make him ready to face his own discomfort. But here is what I can do: I can commit that I will not be the one to use humor to mask painful feelings, and I certainly will not be the one to use humor against others, even though it's tempting. It's my job to resist the temptation because it's the courageous and compassionate thing to do. But it's hard.

Recently, a friend of mine called me to vent some frustration about her difficulty getting pregnant. The doctor told her and her husband, Tim, that stress may be a factor. She called me about a month ago, and I can distinctly remember her saying, "Stress? Like, are you fucking kidding me? It's not like my stress is ever going away. I work insane hours, and my job is really high-pressured. Like, when does my doctor think I'm going to reduce my goddamn stress?"

About two weeks later, she called me to tell me she was laid off from her job. She seemed to be in good spirits about it, so I felt tempted to joke, "Awesome! There goes your stress! Time to get knocked up!" The more courageous thing to do was acknowledge all the challenges before her. Instead of making the joke, I said, "You seem like you're handling this with a positive attitude. Does that feel like what you need?"

She said, "Uh . . . can you hang on a second?" She went silent for about fifteen or twenty seconds, and then she returned to say, "Sorry, I'm trying to be upbeat for Tim, and he was in the room a minute ago. Big changes really freak him out. Now that it's just you and me, Kate, I'll tell you, I'm terrified that he's going to say we should stop trying to have a baby because we only have one income now. I want to keep trying."

That I had resisted the urge to be funny was such a relief. She already had one person in her life (Tim) who was requiring her to be peppy and positive. I was lucky enough to be the friend who received her authenticity rather than her fake positivity. Actually, luck had nothing to do with it. I earned her authentic feelings because I proved I could sit with negativity without looking away or diverting attention with humor.

If you're like me and you grew up in a family that would make jokes to smooth over difficult feelings and moments of vulnerability, you'll be just as tempted as I was to make pain-relieving jokes, but resist the urge whenever possible. Let's put humor through the four standards to see what we can learn.

Standard #1: Listen More Than You Speak

Humor is only functional when all parties of the conversation are in on the joke. This can require careful listening between two people. Let me give an example from my own work as a professional workshop facilitator. About five or six years ago, I delivered a training for a group of healthcare providers within a large hospital system. I was tasked with training them in patient-centered communication styles.

Everything went wrong that day. The air conditioner broke, so the room was uncomfortably hot. The host forgot to bring a projector, so I could not share my power point slides. There was a heavy traffic jam on the local highway, so half of the participants were late arriving. The maintenance staff spilled coffee all over my handouts. They were ruined. The nearest bathroom was under construction. And due to some patient emergencies, several participants had to leave early. It was a mess.

By the end of the day, I was exhausted. I stopped at the hotel bar for a relaxing glass of wine before retiring to my room, and I called my friend Sarah to tell her about my day. After I explained the series of unfortunate incidents, Sarah laughed so hard and said, "Well, they're going to have your picture up on the wall to warn people before you come back next time!"

I laughed a little, but I added, "Well, none of it was my fault!"

Sarah continued to poke fun at me, "They are going to run for the hills next time your name pops up!"

We went several rounds like this. Obviously, she was just having a little fun at my expense, but I felt like we were laughing at different things. I was tired, annoyed about my day, and only interested in laughing at the disorganization of the hospital leadership team. I wasn't in a good place to laugh at myself, and Sarah wasn't listening closely enough to understand that from my words. It was, of course, well-meaning humor, but it wasn't helping me laugh my bad day away. Instead, I felt a little regretful that I had called her at all.

Standard #2: Assert and Respect Boundaries

I used to work as a victim advocate in a busy emergency room. It was my job to support patients who had been victims of sexual assault and domestic violence. One day, I was sitting with a patient—let's call her Angie—when her doctor entered the room to check on her status. He charged in playfully, "Hiya, Angie! How's it going in here, gals?" It was my job to follow Angie's lead, and she was not amused. So we both stared at him stoically. Dr. Goofball was relentless. He loudly asked, "How was your vaginal exam? I hope my fingers aren't too big!" He laughed at his own joke while I sat there, stunned, and Angie was re-traumatized. I'm sure it was uncomfortable for Dr. Goofball to meet Angie in her moment of tragedy, but he did more harm by cracking jokes. Later, I met with my clinical supervisor to tell her about the encounter, and her response was clear: "To a rape victim, that was verbal violence."

I can't think of a worse time to violate someone's boundaries. When you're trying to help someone, let them draw the lines of the conversation. Let them decide how much humor is welcome. Dr. Goofball was only concerned with breaking the tension in the room. Angie and I preferred the tension over the torturous comedy act.

Standard #3: Forgive Yourself for Not Reading Minds

There will be moments when you feel pretty sure that some comic relief would be helpful, and other times it's impossible to read the room for confirmation. As we've been saying for several chapters now, you cannot read minds. So when you're unsure about the timing of your humor or whether it is appropriate, exercise caution. Tread lightly and be ready to apologize without being defensive or blaming. To say, "Oh, come on, chill out. It was just a joke!" is not an acceptable apology. Dr. Goofball certainly did not read the room.

Standard #4: Embrace Vulnerability

Humor often disguises anxiety or discomfort when people feel vulnerable. I think that was the case with my friend Ravi. He reached out to me when he was feeling down, and then he immediately felt vulnerable, so he quickly turned to humor to protect himself. He put his armor on. The same was true for Dr. Goofball. He was a man, facing a woman who had been violently injured by a man. He felt uncomfortable- maybe even ashamed in some way. His humor was his armor.

To face hard truths without humor or distraction is true intimacy. When you realize you can tell someone your truth, when you can show yourself to them, when you can stand in front of them and their response is "you're safe with me"—that's intimacy. If you get the chance to do that for someone, take it. If you find, in a sort of ironic way, that withholding humor brings you joy, let it.

I have found that humor can be downright vicious. This may be especially true for sarcasm, which psychologists and sociologists view as rooted in unresolved anger or insecurity (Nilsen and Nilsen, 2018, p. 304). I have also found that exceptionally clever jokes can exert power over a conversation, as if the jokester is flexing the brain muscle in front of minds he perceives as weaker than his own. It seems to be a display of intellect, which might come across like one-upping a person. I can think of times when I was trying to have a serious conversation and a person kept making jokes, leaving me to think, *He's scrapping for control and power here. I will not fight him for it.* In that regard, humor can be weaponized to show others your intellectual strength, but there is another option. You could, instead, show your emotional strength.

I recall taking part in a board meeting for a nonprofit organization in Chicago when the chair introduced a new employee who was young, eager, and very engaged. However, I noticed that whenever he made a comment, one of the older board members would turn his legitimate comment into a joke. I imagined how that could drive an otherwise engaged employee into quiet submission out of fear of being humiliated. I brought the issue to the chair and vice chair, discussing the role we have in making sure everyone feels psychologically supported. I said, "No one is a joke here, and I hope you agree."

Chapter 7:

Well-Meaning Gift Giving

The meaning of life is to find your gift.
The purpose of life is to give it away.
—Pablo Picasso

There is a small convenience store near my home in Philadelphia. In between appointments or errands, I can run over to the store and grab small items I need, making it back in the same time it takes to brew a cup of coffee. It's one of the great things about living in a city. You can run out of your home in sweatpants, slippers, and curlers (bra optional); pick up a few household items; and be home in six minutes. My mother wouldn't approve, but the city of Philadelphia does.

One day, while lightly jogging across the street to the store, I noticed a man sitting outside the entrance to the shop. He looked like he hadn't showered in weeks, and my assumption was that he was homeless and needed care. Without breaking my stride, I pointed to the man and said, "Hey, friend, you need anything inside?" I expected him to bounce back quickly, "Some juice and a couple of bananas please!" while I just kept running by, but instead, he put his wrinkled and worn hand up like a stop sign. I paused my jog and waited, confused. He looked at me with concern in his eyes—concern *for me*. He said, "Wait, how are you doing today? Are you okay?"

Still confused, I said, "I'm fine. You need anything inside the store?"

He crinkled his eyes and wrinkled his mouth like he pitied me and adored me simultaneously. He said, "Nice to meet you, neighbor. I'm John. What's your name?"

This man was doing something so rare I couldn't even recognize it: He was being kind. I relaxed my shoulders, unclenched my jaw, and leaned into the moment. "I'm Kate."

He pressed again, "Are you okay, Kate? You're running awfully fast."

Truthfully, I really didn't know why I had been running. I wasn't in a hurry, and nothing was wrong, but he deserved more than "I'm fine, thanks." So I told him about my day. I told him how excited I was to visit my friends over the weekend and about my favorite doughnut shops and how I really enjoy cooking meals that fit into one pot. He told me he hoped the Eagles would win the game later today and that he missed going to the Jersey Shore like he did when he was a kid. We both enjoyed a moment of humanity for a second. Every time I felt tempted to cut the conversation short, I reminded myself that this man, even though he doesn't have an address, is my neighbor. He is not a cup for me to throw loose coins into.

After a few minutes, I said, "John, I'm going inside the store, and I'd be happy to pick something up for you."

He responded, "That's really kind, Kate. There isn't much I need, but I'm wondering if they have a pair of socks inside. Mine have a hole."

I promised to look for the socks, but I had never shopped for socks in a convenience store before, so I wasn't confident that I'd deliver. But right next to the motorcycle magazines and chewing tobacco was a six-pack of men's socks. The manager must know his target market for convenient store socks: men.

I also bought him some juice and bananas. It was a small price to pay for the important lesson John taught me that day: Different people like to receive gifts in different ways. For John, socks were nice, but he needed a neighbor more. My offer to buy him something was coming from a good place, but it was not the gift he needed most.

You've been there. I'm sure you have received a gift that you knew was well meant, but it wasn't what you really wanted, needed, or expected.

Maybe the gift made no sense, or it was insulting, or it posed an inconvenience for you.

I once received a tomato plant that would not stop growing, and I lived in a city apartment with no balcony. I honestly think the amount it grew just sitting in my living room defied science. It was, at best, an odd gift to give a person who lives in an apartment with no outdoor space and, at worst, a complete disregard of my lifestyle. I mean, I am on the road every single week. Who the hell is supposed to water this thing?

I actually polled the *Only Trying to Help* podcast followers to get some feedback about gift giving. I asked folks to tell me about a time they had received a gift that was insulting, and I don't think I have ever laughed so hard. Some examples were incredible.

1. Hygiene or hair removal products
2. Underwear (one person specifically noted that she received underwear designed to hide a "muffin top")
3. A book about repairing relationships (in this case, a man gifted the book to his own girlfriend, but I'm not sure that detail matters)
4. A book with instructions for having appropriate workplace relationships
5. Inappropriately sized clothing (too big or too small)
6. Various items that suggest the gift receiver needs to lose weight

Obviously, the world needs some guidance about gift giving. Let's walk through those four standards.

Standard #1: Listen More Than You Speak

My mom loves a sale, and she's perfectly happy to share her frugal finds with the people she loves. So she'll find some product I enjoy—my favorite pasta sauce or boxes of Raisinets candy—and she'll show up to my house with twenty-five of them. And believe me, I know how lucky I am to have a parent who does things like that. But once she made a habit out of it, I had to tell her I don't have space in my tiny, little South Philly home to store all this stuff.

"Mom, this is so nice of you, but you have to stop because I'm stepping over this stuff to get through my living room. I feel like a hoarder."

"But you like it! And there is no reason to pay full price for these things!"

"But, Mom, I don't have the luxury of storage space that you have. This is posing an inconvenience, and I know you don't want that."

"But you don't find the sales I find!"

It's hard for her to shift her mindset. She values a sale as much as I value having a tidy home free of clutter. Sometimes I'm left feeling like she just isn't listening to me and my values. Of course, it's tough to stay mad when I'm indulging in chocolate and pasta all the time, and I will certainly miss stepping over those piles of groceries someday when she is gone.

Standard #2: Assert and Respect Boundaries

There are unspoken rules about the boundaries of gift giving. It's not, for example, appropriate to give your mother-in-law lingerie or to buy your boss something extravagant like a car or a yacht. It's also inappropriate to give a gift than ends up costing the receiver time or money.

I learned that lesson during Christmastime, when I was fifteen years old. That year, I had my first real job—not babysitting, not taking care of someone's plants or pets—a job with a time clock and taxes. I was, for the first time in my life, receiving a steady paycheck, and when Christmastime arrived, I was elated to have money for gifts. Until then, my gifts were either homemade or purchased at the school holiday craft fair, where items cost two or three dollars. Suddenly, I had a few hundred dollars in my bank account, and I was prepared to spend it all on gifts. I bought my mom an electronic car starter, which was pretty groundbreaking technology back then. I liked that she could warm up her car while she drank her morning coffee. I got my dad tickets to see a Broadway show called *It Ain't Nothin' But the Blues*. It was such a memorable trip because we traveled to New York City, stayed in a hotel in Times Square, saw the tree at Rockefeller Center, walked around Central Park, and ate sandwiches from a classic New York deli. It wasn't until we were already in New York, having the time of our lives, that I realized my "gift" cost him a lot of money. He never complained once. I think he was giving me a break because I was still a kid, but as an adult, I try hard not to repeat this mistake.

I like to think I learned my lesson about that, so years later, when my sister was pregnant and I wanted to gift her a prenatal massage, I thought to myself, *This is going to be a hassle for her because she'll have to find a babysitter for her one-year-old, and I know I can't volunteer because I'm traveling for work.* So I made sure I called my parents and secured them as babysitters before I scheduled it. I didn't want the gift to pose a cost or an inconvenience to her.

Remember "guessing and asking"? Respecting boundaries requires us to be good at both. It might sound like these:

- "I would like to treat you and your husband to a night out. If I planned something, would you have any concerns about that?"
- "I would normally buy you something silly for your birthday, but given the year you've had, I'm guessing you might prefer an outing like a dinner or a movie. I can come up with the plans, but am I on the right track?"
- "I baked muffins, and I would like to bring them over. I'm guessing I could leave them at your door. Do you have any objections or concerns? I could come another time, or I could skip it entirely, if that's better."

Guessing and asking allows the receiver to say, "I won't be home later. Please leave the muffins with my neighbor" or "Muffins sound great, but I'm allergic to nuts."

Standard #3: Forgive Yourself for Not Reading Minds

The best gifts are the ones that show me how well you know me. I don't expect anyone to read my mind, but I hope that a gift makes me say aloud, *Wow, you totally get me.* Unfortunately, I still sometimes receive a gift that makes me ask, *Do you even know me at all?*

I'm a vegetarian, but for years, my parents would take me to a steakhouse on my birthday. I had a friend who gave me tickets to see *her* favorite band. This is really common because, in lieu of reading minds, we tend to show love to people in the same way we like to receive love.

Gary Chapman wrote about this in his landmark 1995 book *The Five Love Languages*. It seemed like half the planet read that book, yet we continue to mess this up. Chapman told us that everyone speaks a love language. Some of us like to show and receive love through quality time, while others prefer to show and receive love through acts of service, words of affirmation, physical touch, or tangible gifts. Show people you know them well by speaking *their* love language, not just your own.

If your friend's love language is quality time, try giving a gift that involves doing something together, like reservations for a wine tasting or tickets to a baseball game. If your child's love language is physical touch, try snuggling up and watching a movie. If your colleague's love language is acts of service, try offering to pick up their morning coffee at Starbucks to save them the trip.

About a year ago, I lost my bags during a flight from Newark to Greenville, and I called my best friend Julie to vent my frustration. She had the most generous response. She said, "Would you like me to wait on the phone line with the airline so you can get other stuff done?" I couldn't allow her to do that because it felt like too large of a gift to me, but I proceeded to call other people and brag about my kick-ass friend and the act of service she offered in my time of need. My bags could wait.

Unfortunately, we don't do a good job of speaking another person's love language. We give love the way we like to receive it. I recall being in a relationship with a man who always promised cuddles when I was having a bad day. That was his love language, but it wasn't mine. I thrive on hearing words of affirmation, so I wanted to hear, "You had a horrible day, and you crushed it, Kate. I'm so proud of you for conquering Mount Everest today." But physical touch was his love language, so that's all he could think to offer. He would always say, "I will give you a big hug later!"

Here's the kicker: Our love language is likely to be something that was lacking in our childhood. To you, it might just be a hug or a note or a chore, but to the person on the receiving end, it could be the exact thing they've been waiting for their entire lives. It might make no sense to you, but the point is to speak the *other* person's language. You're touching their heart in a way that, apparently, others could not in the past.

Standard #4: Embrace Vulnerability

Gift giving is inherently vulnerable. *What if my gift makes someone uncomfortable? What if they don't like it? What if they already have it? What if my gift is too much or too little?* Well, vulnerability is all about putting yourself out there. I try to remember that at Christmastime. We're all gathered around in a living room, fire crackling and cookies baking, meanwhile hoping that everyone likes the gifts. It's risky and thrilling and terrifying, and more than anything, it's an enormous act of vulnerability.

Even though I tease my mom about her penchant for binge-buying my favorite items, I cannot end this chapter without honoring her as one of the best gift givers I know. Even if she gives a gift certificate or a bottle of wine, she attaches a funny poem to each one. She also has the capacity to be very giving of her resources and her time. I recall being in the car with her when I was a child and she saw an elderly man carrying groceries away from the grocery store alone. It had to be 90 degrees and humid in the Northeast, and it was no environment for an old man to be walking around outside.

Without hesitation, she pulled the car over to the side of busy West Chester Pike in Delaware County, Pennsylvania, and while loud cars zoomed by, she shouted out the window, "Sir, may I please drive you home?" She let a stranger into the car with her and her two young daughters because she couldn't live with herself if she let him walk home with those bags of food. Now *that's* a gift. She didn't *need* to open herself to the vulnerability of having a stranger in her car, but she was courageous and kind enough to do it anyway. She improved his life that day. That's just who she is.

Chapter 8:

Well-Meaning Lies

The great enemy of truth is very often not the lie—deliberate, contrived and dishonest—but the myth, persistent, persuasive and unrealistic. Too often we hold fast to the clichés of our forebears. We subject all facts to a prefabricated set of interpretations. We enjoy the comfort of opinion without the discomfort of thought.
—President John F. Kennedy

This will not be an overly self-righteous speech about the value of honesty. In fact, I'm not entirely convinced that honesty is always the best policy, and readers could easily accuse me of hypocrisy if I were to preach about living with sincerity and integrity. I haven't done so. We've all learned over the course of our lives that sometimes a small lie helps. It can help us avoid an awkward conversation, it can help us avoid hurting someone's feelings, and it can reduce our deep personal shame (like when I lie to myself about still looking great in my high school prom dress). Sometimes no one is harmed.

Of course, there are also times when a lie—even a well-intentioned one—will perpetuate a myth or a cultural norm that stigmatizes an otherwise harmless behavior. In fact, I worry a great deal that our lies protect and embolden hidden messages that are harmful to society.

For example, when I was conducting a training workshop about two years ago, one participant stood up in the middle of our session and announced to the room, "I will be right back. I just need to make a phone call." Most of us were perfectly happy to carry on in her absence. But before

I could move forward with the agenda, she gestured for me to come closer to her, and then, standing there near the exit, she whispered, "Sorry, I have to go breastfeed." I gave her a quick nod, and she was out the door.

Frankly, it's none of our business what she does when she leaves the room. She could have left without an announcement at all, but since she bothered to make one, I also think she could have been honest. That is obviously her decision to make, but I suppose I'm optimistic for a world where women can feed their babies without having to lie about it. Call me a romantic, if you want.

Had a child been observing our whispered exchange by the door, the child might have learned that breastfeeding is bad or shameful. The message: Breastfeeding is not something to be honest about. It's lie-worthy or whisper-worthy. I really believe that we grow up to lie about the things we witnessed our parents lie about years ago. It's passed from generation to generation. Even with the best of intentions, we can spread messages about which truths are acceptable in the world and which truths we need to hide.

Let's walk through the four standards to explore more about well-meant lies.

Standard #1: Listen More Than You Speak

I recently spoke to someone who took ballet lessons as a child, and when she put on the tights and leotard for the very first time, her mom said, "Don't worry, we'll get you a skirt to cover up your thighs. No one has to know why. That will be our secret." That's when she learned that her thighs were unacceptable and that they should be hidden from others. She was five years old, and before her mother offered to lie for her, she had no idea there was anything wrong with her thighs. She had, until that point, enjoyed five precious years of a positive body image, and it came crashing down that day when she learned that she might be difficult for others to see.

In this scenario, the mother didn't ask, "How do you feel in your leotard, dear?" She didn't listen to her daughter's worries or celebrations, her shame, or her pride. She just started talking.

Before you offer to lie on someone's behalf—thinking that you're helping the person—please take a moment to listen first. You might find out that this person is not interested in your lie or sees no reason for the lie in the first place.

Standard #2: Assert and Respect Boundaries

I can think of a time when I was invited to a cocktail party. It wasn't particularly important that I attend. It wasn't my parent's fiftieth wedding anniversary or my best friend's engagement party. It was just another cocktail party like a million others I've been invited to over the years. Since I was tired from having traveled a lot, I decided to RSVP no. But instead of saying with honesty "I'm just too tired to socialize after so much travel," I created a complicated story about why I couldn't attend. I don't know why I did that. It was so unnecessary.

I said, "Well, I really haven't been feeling well, and I'm concerned that I might be contagious and make other people sick. Plus, I have an early morning the next day, and I haven't been sleeping well, so I ought to get some rest. And now that I think about it, I have some paperwork to catch up on for a big meeting coming up. It's just a lot of things, and I have to get focused right now."

It was as silly as it was complicated, and ultimately, it required me to remember all the details of this lie the next time I saw this person face-to-face. I don't know why I think it matters so much that I have an elaborate story. No one cares. I'm not really that important to the success of the cocktail party. People will still have fun without me, and most won't even notice my absence. Why do I put myself through this?

Sometimes we lie because we are avoiding setting a boundary. It's just easier to lie than to assert our needs. This can be rooted in the deep belief that we are not worthy of rest and self-care.

A few years ago, I heard a similar story from someone who attended one of my lectures. We had been speaking about self-care and boundaries when an audience member walked to the standing microphone and said this about her family:

"Growing up, my dad would say that he was cleaning the garage, but he was really watching the football game on a small TV out there and drinking a few beers. My mom would claim to be cleaning the bathroom, but she would sit in there reading romance novels and sipping rosé. And that's how I learned that I don't have the right to be alone or to practice self-care without lying about it. They taught me that being kind to yourself is not okay, but lying is."

For that reason, I'd encourage you to be careful what you lie about and what you whisper about in front of your children. They may become injured bystanders. When children hear their parents lie or whisper about certain topics, they receive the message that the topic is bad. These are unintended consequences, but consequences nonetheless. Let your children catch you in the act of boundary-setting, not lying.

Standard #3: Forgive Yourself for Not Reading Minds

In my twenties, I worked with a woman named Monique. We were good friends. We spent time together outside of work. We knew each other's families, and we shared personal stories with each other. She wasn't just another colleague to me. One day at work, Monique was in a terrible mood and everyone could tell. Folks were asking me, "What's up with her? Do you know?" I didn't. Later, when we were alone in a conference room, I checked in with her and asked, "Hey, is everything okay? You don't seem yourself." She broke down in tears. I shut the door of the conference room, hoping to offer her more privacy, and then I sat next to her. She had difficulty speaking through her tears, but she slowly spurted out, "I ... had ... a ... mis ... carriage."

There was my friend, naked with her emotions. She was feeling pain and allowing herself to show it. I took a deep inhale to my belly, held it for a second, and pushed it out. With that release, I said, "Okay. I'm the only one who knows, and when they ask me what's wrong, I will tell them you're just not feeling well. No one needs to know the truth, okay? It's safe with me. *You* are safe with me."

She stopped crying—not because she felt better, but because I think her emotions shifted from sadness to annoyance. With big, stern eyes, she looked at me and said, "There is nothing to hide. I'm not ashamed."

Of course. Of course! Why should she be ashamed? Why did I assume she would want me to hide this information? What have I learned and internalized about miscarriages that made me believe this was inherently shameful?

The incredible thing about it is that I would have thought better of myself. I would have thought I'd be the one to say, "There is no shame in a miscarriage." This bias that I had against miscarriages was beneath my awareness. That's how biases work. They lurk in the ugly parts of our minds. We don't even know they're there. Biases hide so we can lie to ourselves and tell ourselves how good we are, how open-minded we are, how progressive we are, and how sensitive we are to the needs of others.

Then I projected my bias onto Monique, assuming that she was feeling the same way I felt about it. Rather than trying to assume her feelings, I should have inquired about them. I wish I had just asked her what she wanted. I wish I had said something like "Monique, you've clearly told me something that is heavy, and it's yours—not mine—to share. If anyone asks me about your low mood today, what would you like me to say? I could tell them the truth, I could suggest they speak to you directly, or I could say any other thing that you might prefer. What do you think?" I can't know until she tells me.

Standard #4: Embrace Vulnerability

Being truthful comes with risks, and it makes us feel vulnerable to potential ridicule and shame. I often collaborate with a therapist who always says, "Clients lie to me all the time. Rather than calling them out on their lies, I try to understand how the lie protects them. How does the lie reduce their vulnerability?" Brilliant.

I know a gentleman named Adam who lost his job recently. He told me how hurtful it was to hear his wife lie on his behalf. He overheard her telling her friends, "Oh, Adam has had so many job offers, but he's being picky because he's seizing this opportunity to grow and chase his dreams." Not true. He hadn't had a single job offer. He didn't even really have career dreams, he admitted to me. He also overheard his wife tell the neighbors he quit his job rather than the truth: The company laid him off. Adam told me how much it hurt him to hear her lie. He asked me, "Is it really so bad to be unemployed, Kate? Is it really that awful if people know the truth? I am a good person, and I have done nothing wrong." He felt offended, and he was neither on the receiving end nor the deliverer of that lie. He was an injured bystander. Likely, Adam's wife was guarding against judgmental people. She put her armor on.

So I might suggest that the next time you are about to lie, even if no one would ever know about it, reflect on why you feel the need to lie at all. Ask yourself, "What has society taught me about this? Did I learn somewhere along the way that this is shameful or inappropriate? And is that the right message? Who benefits when I spread that message? Do I want to perpetuate that secrecy of this topic? Or do I want to break that cycle moving forward?" You get to choose.

Conclusion

*I hope you never lose yourself trying to love someone else.
It's a long way back.
—Stephanie Bennett-Henry*

Only Trying to Help is just a book about how to love people better by honoring your relationships above all else. One podcast listener said to me, "Oh my god, I feel like you're making me a better person." But let me be clear—this book was about being a better *helper*, not a better *person*. I knew all along that my readers and listeners are good people. But part of the danger of believing in the false dichotomy of "good people" and "bad people" is that "good people" are so invested in being "good" that they have trouble acknowledging the harm they may have caused while trying to help others. We all mess up, my friends—even if you're woke, even if you're a social worker, and even if you're a genius. This book is full of stories about people (myself included) messing up. But I'm signing up for the lifelong journey of always growing and improving myself because I know I cannot change other people, but I can help other people by changing my behavior when I'm with them. Let me say that again—I cannot change other people, but I can help other people by changing my behavior when I'm with them.

So please own your errors and be better every day because, honestly, the most exhausting people are the ones who need constant reassurance that they're still "good." You don't need to be perfect. What's important is owning your mistakes, learning from them, and being better in the future. You have so much love in your heart for others—you might as well save some for yourself while you're doing all this hard work. This shit ain't for the weak. If you're tempted to just say, "Eff it. It's too hard. I am who I am," please remember adults have a responsibility to figure out which traits are toxic and hurtful. Maturity is knowing that you're sometimes part of the problem. It sucks, but at least there's wine.

It's okay to take some breaks and share the work with others because you're not the only helper on the planet. The Talmud states, "Do not be daunted by the enormity of the world's grief. Do justly now, love mercifully now, walk humbly now. You are not obligated to complete the work, but neither are you free to abandon it." Or as I like to put it, just do your part. Be gentle with yourself because it's difficult to be present for the liberation of others who are in pain.

When you're the one who is in need, may the bartenders and barbershop owners in your own life be there for you as they were for me.

Afterword:

Publishing in the COVID Era

I wrote and edited most of this book during the 2020 COVID-19 outbreak in the United States and around the world. Times of disaster have a way of bringing out the best and worst of humanity. While there were heartwarming examples of courage, brotherly love, and survival, there were also ugly tales of robbery, greed, and competition.

Personally, I had just returned from a trip to Cuba, and I decided that I ought to self-quarantine for at least fourteen days, not sure if I had unknowingly picked up the virus in one of the many airports I had visited along my journey. So at home and isolated, I poured out a few hundred pages of thoughts on helpfulness. In the background, my TV showed images of stores being looted, people hoarding toilet paper, and the economy crashing. Countries had closed their borders, entire communities were on lockdown, and people were suffering on every continent. Anxieties were running high. There was so much to worry about:

- *Will my mom and dad be okay?*
- *Does my sister have enough formula and diapers for my niece and nephew?*
- *When will the economy recover?*
- *Will my business collapse?*
- *Will food stores run out of supplies?*
- *What if someone breaks into my house to steal my supplies?*
- *Will pharmacies close?*
- *Will essential first responders fall ill?*
- *How long will this last?*

- *If someone I love gets sick, will I be able to visit them in the hospital? What if they die? Will we be able to have a funeral?*

I can't tell you how healing it was for me to turn to my computer and write page after page about the possibilities of compassion, empathy, and kindness that exist among us. I limited myself to one or two hours of news coverage daily and then spent the rest of the day imagining stories of love and service. What a gift this book was to me during that time. Even now, as I write this paragraph, I am thinking to myself, even if I don't sell a single copy, this was worth my efforts. Writing this book was an exercise in protecting my own mental health during a crisis. It's hard to imagine what might have happened to my heart had I not been able to keep it so warm.

Resources

Brown, Brené Brown. *Daring Greatly: How the Courage to be Vulnerable Transforms the Way We Live, Love, Parent and Lead.* 2013.

Chapman, Gary. *The Five Love Languages: How to Express Heartfelt Commitment to Your Mate.* Chicago: Northfield, 1995.

Claiborne, Shane, Jonathan Wilson-Hartgrove, and Enuma Okoro. *Common Prayer: A Liturgy for Ordinary Radicals.* Grand Rapids, MI: Zondervan, 2010.

Eichler, A. "Askers vs. Guessers." *The Atlantic*, May 12, 2010. Accessed on November 24, 2020: https://www.theatlantic.com/national/archive/2010/05/askers-vs-guessers/340891/.

Epley, Nicholas. *Mindwise: How We Understand What Others Think, Believe, Feel, and Want.* 2014.

Falk, Emily, Matthew O'Donnell, Christopher Cascio, Francis Tinney, Yoona Kang, Matthew Lieberman, Shelley Taylor, Lawrence A, Ken Resnicow, and Victor Strecher. "Self-affirmation Alters the Brain's Response to Health Messages and Subsequent Behavior Change. *Proceedings of the National Academy of Sciences* 112, no. 7 (2015): 1977–82. doi: 10.1073/pnas.1500247112.

Farber, Sharon. "The Tragic Side of Comedy, Where the Pain Lives." *Psychology Today*, September 9, 2014.

https://www.psychologytoday.com/us/blog/the-mind-body-connection/201409/the-tragic-side-comedy-where-the-pain-lives.

Force, Nichole. "Humor as Weapon, Shield and Psychological Salve." Psych Central, 2018. Retrieved on April 30, 2020, from https://psychcentral.com/lib/humor-as-weapon-shield-and-psychological-salve/.

hooks, bell. *The Will to Change: Men, Masculinity, and Love* (2004), 66.

Kohlrieser, George. "Unleash Potential as a Secure Base Leader." https://www.georgekohlrieser.com (accessed February 16, 2021).

Moyers, Theresa, and William Miller. (2013). "Is Low Therapist Empathy Toxic?" *Psychology of Addictive Behaviors* 27, no. 3 (2013), 878–884.

Nilsen, Don, and Alleen Nilsen. *The Language of Humor: An Introduction.* Cambridge: Cambridge University Press, 2018.

Stein, Garth. *The Art of Racing in the Rain: A Novel.* New York: Harper, 2009.

Stewart, Simon, and David Thompson. "Does Comedy Kill? A Retrospective, Longitudinal Cohort, Nested Case-Control Study of Humour and Longevity in 53 British Comedians." *International Journal of Cardiology* 180 (2015): 258–61. doi: 10.1016/j.ijcard.2014.11.152.

Sue, Derald, Christina Capodilupo, Gina Torino, Jennifer Bucceri, Aisha Holder, Kevin Nadal, and Marta Esquilin. "Racial Microaggressions in Everyday Life: Implications for Clinical Practice." *American Psychologist* 62, no. 4 (2007), 271–286. https://doi.org/10.1037/0003-066X.62.4.271

Sunstein, Cass. "In Politics, Apologies Are for Losers." *New York Times*, July 27, 2019.

Appendix A:
Tips for Effective Self-Disclosure

Sometimes helpers believe it is useful to talk about their own experiences. We call this self-disclosure because the helper is speaking about himself or herself. Self-disclosure can be problematic because it robs the attention from the person you're trying to help, it dismisses the speaker's point, and it might put the person you're trying to help in a difficult position of needing to support you, the helper.

Sometimes people write to me and ask, "Well, if I don't talk about my own experiences, what else can I talk about?" The answer is simple: Listen more. When your friend or sister or colleague gets quiet, show more interest by asking them to elaborate. Rather than saying "Oh, that happened to me once," try asking a question like "Wow. What was that like?" or "What made you do that?"

But if you are still considering self-disclosure, follow these steps to be more effective and reduce potential harm:

1. Ask yourself, are you sharing your story to help the other person, or are you sharing your story because it feels good to YOU? If you are truly sharing with the other person's best interest in mind, proceed to number 2. If the self-disclosure is more for your own benefit, please refrain from acting on your urge to share.

2. If you really want to share something, ask for permission to do so. You might say something like "So I'm listening to your story, and it reminds me of something I went through. I'm tempted to share it, but I want to make sure you're done sharing because I don't want to interrupt. Is this a good time?"

3. Be humble. You are sharing your own thoughts, experiences, and feelings—not hard science. The person you are speaking to does not need to accept your story as truth. You might say something like "Well, I'm only one person, but based on my experience . . ."

Perform this three-step check and you are likely to reduce the number of times you accidentally steal the attention from the person you're trying to help.

Appendix B:
Examples of Boundaries

Boundaries separate what belongs to me from what belongs to you. Imagine boundaries surround you like a physical fence or a wall. Some people have a very permeable boundary. It's too flexible. It's like a wiry or broken fence. Everything gets in. They don't assert or protect their boundaries. Others have a brick wall with no way in. These people are closed off and rigid. They have strict rules, and they often avoid intimate relationships with others. This can be a lonely life. The ideal boundary is a sturdy fence with a gate. The owner of the boundary decides when to open the gate and when to close it. The owner of the boundary would ideally only open the gate out of love and a deep desire to help the person, not out of fear of consequence or punishment.

This becomes a lot more complicated in relationships, where one person's boundaries will bump up against another person's boundaries. We may not agree on what belongs to me and what belongs to you, and we still have to negotiate the best way to behave. Sometimes a person with rigid boundaries meets someone with permeable boundaries or vice versa. Depending on the scenario, a few things are possible.

One possibility is that boundaries are respected. In this case, neither party tramples on the boundaries of the other party. When I offer my nephew a hug and he rejects me, I tell him, "That's no problem. Hugs are your choice." I adjust my boundaries to respect his. Adjustments are okay as long as they are motivated by love, not fear.

I know a man who is a CEO of a midsize firm. His team meetings always run long, and he attributes the problem to "people who won't shut up." When I ask him why he doesn't just end the meeting, he says, "I don't want to make people mad." He adjusts his own schedule to accommodate the never-ending meetings because he is afraid of a consequence from his staff. He is motivated by fear.

Sometimes we spend a lot of money on birthday gifts for children because we are motivated by our love and our joy of giving. Other times we spend a lot of money on birthday gifts for children because we fear they will be disappointed.

Sometimes we work late, motivated by the joy we feel from accomplishment. Other times we work late, motivated by the fear of getting fired.

We've covered situations when boundaries are respected and when boundaries are adjusted. Sometimes, however, boundaries are downright violated. When I'm giving a professional presentation to a large audience and during the question-and-answer session, a person asks, "How old are you?" or "Are you married?" that person is storming through my fence. I hadn't opened the door, and my boundaries were breached.

Then there are times when we are allowing our boundaries to be violated. I had a client say to me, "My wife makes me do all the housework! I'm sick of it."

"How?" I asked.

He said, "Well, she gets upset, and it turns into a big argument, and it's just not worth it, so I do the housework."

"So you're weighing the options of (a) defending your boundaries with an argument or (b) letting her violate your boundaries to keep the peace. That's a decision that *you* are making, and lately, you've decided to skip the argument, sacrifice your boundaries, and gain peace in exchange. That's fine. You can do that. Or you can choose to assert the boundary. It's really your choice, but know that YOU make that choice, not your wife. If only 50 percent of the housework gets done because she refuses to meet you halfway, that is her choice as well."

I'm suspicious anytime a person uses this pattern of speech: "_____ always makes me _____." Here are some examples: *My wife always makes* me buy her flowers. *My son always makes me give him dessert. My neighbor always makes me lend him my lawn mower.* My favorite is *My wife made me buy her* Hamilton *tickets for $2,000!*

Excuse me? They "made you"? Exactly how does a person make you do something? Did they put a gun to your head? I think not. When a person says, "My ex is making me give her the cat," they mean "My ex is demanding the cat, and I'm allowing it to happen." Children don't make you buy toys at the store or stay at the pool longer than you intended or give them junk food for dinner. You are an autonomous adult, and you may be struggling with boundaries. It's okay to adjust your boundaries from time to time, but for crying out loud, make sure your adjustment is motivated by joy. Go ahead and give your kid dessert, but do it because you LOVE seeing the smile on her face, not because you're afraid of a tantrum. There is a difference.

How you set your boundaries sends a message to the world about how you respect yourself. Learning to assert your own boundaries often makes it easier to recognize and respect the boundaries that other people set. When someone sends me a text that says, "Hey, sorry to cancel plans for tonight, but I have a lot going on," I think to myself, *Nice boundaries, dude. Well done.* It's so much easier for me to respect the lines that people draw when I have practiced drawing them myself. It takes one to know one, right?

The next time someone cancels plans with you, try responding with something like "You made the right call. I know that's tough to do." It's freeing to not be so resentful. The world teaches us we're supposed to feel slighted when someone sets a boundary with us. It's possible to be disappointed and proud at the same time. You might even use that as your response. You could say, "I'm disappointed that I won't get to see you but also really proud that you're taking care of yourself tonight. Looking forward to the next time we can get together. Be well."

You'll know that you're getting better at setting boundaries when you find yourself attracted to other people who set boundaries well. You might find that you're less interested in spending time with the people who struggle with boundaries. They will become frustrating for you. You'll want to surround yourself with people who are good at this, just like you are. Remember, the only people who get mad when you set your boundaries are the people who benefited from you having none at all.

Appendix C: Emotional Vocabulary

Pleasant feelings

Accepting

Affectionate

Amazed

Animated

Anxious

At ease

Attracted

Blessed

Bold

Brave

Calm

Certain

Challenged

Cheerful

Clever

Comfortable

Confident

Content

Courageous

Curious

Daring

Delighted

Determined

Devoted

Eager

Earnest

Ecstatic

Elated

Encouraged

Energetic

Engrossed

Enthusiastic

Excited

Fascinated

Festive

Fortunate

Free

Glad

Gleeful

Hardy

Hopeful

Important

Inquisitive

Inspired

Intent

Interested

Intrigued

Joyous

Jubilant

Kind

Liberated

Loved

Loving

Lucky

Nosy

Optimistic

Overjoyed

Passionate

Peaceful

Playful

Pleased

Provocative

Quiet

Reassured

Rebellious

Receptive

Relaxed

Reliable

Satisfied

Secure

Sensitive

Serene

Spirited

Sure

Surprised

Tenacious

Tender

Thankful

Thrilled

Touched

Unique

Warm

Wonderful

Difficult / Unpleasant feelings

Aggressive

Alarmed

Alone

Annoyed

Anxious

Appalled

Ashamed

Bad

Bitter

Boiling

Bored

Cold

Cowardly

Cross

Crushed

Deprived

Desolate

Despair

Desperate

Despicable

Detestable

Diminished

Disappointed

Discouraged

Disgusting

Disillusioned

Disinterested

Dismayed

Dissatisfied

Distressed

Distrustful

Dominated

Doubtful

Dull

Embarrassed

Empty

Enraged

Fatigued

Fearful

Forced

Frightened

Frustrated

Fuming

Grief

Guilty

Hateful

Heartbroken

Hesitant

Hostile

Humiliated

In a stew

In despair

Incapable

Incensed

Indecisive

Indignant

Inferior

Inflamed

Infuriated

Injured

Insensitive

Insulting

Irritated

Lifeless

Lonely

Lost

Lousy

Miserable

Misgiving

Nervous

Neutral

Nonchalant

Offended

Panic

Paralyzed

Pathetic

Perplexed

Pessimistic

Powerless

Preoccupied

Provoked

Rejected

Repugnant

Resentful

Reserved

Restless

Scared

Shy

Skeptical

Sore

Sorrowful

Stupefied

Suspicious

Tearful

Tense

Terrible

Terrified

Threatened

Tortured

Tragic

Unbelieving

Uncertain

Uneasy

Unhappy

Unsure

Upset

Useless

Vulnerable

Weary

Worried

Wronged

Appendix D: Microaggressions

In Chapter 2, we covered well-meaning compliments. Some well-meaning compliments are also microaggressions (brief comments which reveal a bias and result in a slight to a vulnerable group of people). Microaggressions can come in many forms:

- Microassault: a blatant verbal or nonverbal attack intended to convey biased sentiments

- Microinsult: unintentional behaviors or verbal comments that convey rudeness or insensitivity or demean a person's racial heritage identity, gender identity, or sexual orientation identity

- Microinvalidation: verbal comments or behaviors that exclude, negate, or dismiss the psychological thoughts, feelings, or experiential reality of the target group

Regardless of how insignificant the comment may seem, microaggressions often result in a dilemma for the victim. First, it's difficult or impossible to prove that a person has insulted you with a brief remark like "You're so articulate." Microaggressions often turn into a clash of realities: victim of the microaggression vs. the offender. It's too easy to just tell a person, "Oh, you're overthinking it." There is often a catch-22 of responding to microaggressions. The victim, unfortunately, must first predict if there will be consequences for speaking up.

Use this worksheet to practice understanding the concept of microaggressions as we learned it in Chapter 2: Well-Meaning Compliments.

1. Leaving the office holiday party, Joe turns to several women in the room and says, "Thanks for putting this together, ladies," as he exits the party. What may have been the intended message of the comment? What is the potential impact of the comment?

2. A man in a wheelchair is coming out of the gym and gets into the front seat of a car when a passerby yells, "Wait! I'll help you with the door!" What may have been the intended message of the comment? What is the potential impact of the comment?

3. A student asks an Asian American classmate (who was born in Kansas), "What country are you from?" What may have been the intended message of the comment? What is the potential impact of the comment?

4. A person said to a black CEO, "You're really a credit to your race! You must be so proud." What may have been the intended message of the comment? What is the potential impact of the comment?

For more information:

Visit www.AdvocacyAcademy.org for training, coaching, and consulting with Dr. Kate Watson.

Visit www.OnlyTryingToHelp.com to listen to the podcast.

For booking inquiries, email: Kate@AdvocacyAcademy.org

About the Author

Dr. Kate Watson earned her bachelor's degree in psychology from Towson University and her graduate degree in psychological counseling from Columbia University. She earned her doctorate in health policy and social justice from Drexel University's Dornsife School of Public Health and a certificate of Diversity and Inclusion from Cornell University.

Today, she is the president and founder of the Advocacy Academy, a Philadelphia-based training, consulting, and coaching company. She is a director emeritus of the Motivational Interviewing Network of Trainers and a current board member of the Lady Parts Collective, a Los Angeles–based theater company specializing in the development of work relevant to women in the United States. Kate is an ongoing consultant to the Department of Defense, the NFL, and major television networks. She has conducted trainings in twenty states, eight countries, and across many fields: health care, education, social services, financial advising, victim advocacy, corrections, etc. Kate trains approximately five thousand to ten thousand people a year. She also coaches individuals on how to be better advocates for people, causes, and communities.

With her friend Leslie Ballway, Kate is the host of Only Trying to Help, a weekly podcast available on Spotify, Apple Podcasts, Audible, and directly through her website: www.OnlyTryingToHelp.com. Follow Kate on Twitter and Instagram using @IwasOTTH.